ATLAS OF HISTORY'S GREATEST

HEROES&
VILLAINS

THE 50 MOST SIGNIFICANT PEOPLE EXPLORED IN WORDS AND MAPS

ATLAS OF HISTORY'S GREATEST

HEROES&
VILLAINS

THE 50 MOST SIGNIFICANT PEOPLE EXPLORED IN WORDS AND MAPS

Howard Watson

METRO BOOKS
New York

METRO BOOKS
New York

An Imprint of Sterling Publishing
387 Park Avenue South
New York, NY 10016

© 2013 by Quantum Publishing Ltd
Illustrations and maps © 2013 by Quantum Publishing Ltd

This 2013 edition published by Metro Books by arrangement with Quantum Books.

Publisher: Sarah Bloxham
Managing Editor: Samantha Warrington
Project Editor: Marilyn Inglis
Copy Editor: Miranda Harrison
Assistant Editor: Jo Morley
Editorial Intern: Rebecca Cave
Production Manager: Rohana Yusof
Design: Natalie Clay, www.styloclay.com
Cartographer: Red Lion Mapping

ISBN 978-1-4351-4189-6

For information about custom editions, special sales, and premium and corporate purchases, please contact Sterling Special Sales at 800-805-5489 or specialsales@sterlingpublishing.com.

Manufactured in Hong Kong
2 4 6 8 10 9 7 5 3 1
www.sterlingpublishing.com

Contents

Introduction

FROM SWASHBUCKLING LEGENDS, STUNNING MILITARY STRATEGISTS, AND INDIVIDUALS WHO DIED WHILE PURSUING THEIR NOBLE PRINCIPLES, TO EGOMANIACAL TYRANTS AND CALLOUS MURDERERS WHO BARELY BLINKED AT THE MASS SLAUGHTER THEY INFLICTED, THIS BOOK HIGHLIGHTS HISTORY'S GREATEST HEROES AND VILLAINS.

These heroes and villains should be worlds apart in personality: the devout, the righteous, and the leaders who would do anything to help their nations are ranged against the despotic, the cruel, and the leaders who would do anything to help themselves. Yet close inspection reveals that these heroes and villains are often no more than two sides of the same coin.

There are at least two perspectives on every conflict, so one person's hero is almost sure to be another's villain. After all, Richard the Lionheart's Crusade to the Holy Land in the defense of Christianity was no doubt seen by both Muslims and Jews as an irreligious and villainous assault upon their own holy lands. The distant descendents of the Mongol emperor Genghis Khan still herald his achievement of creating a vast empire across the whole expanse of Asia as one of the most amazing feats in history; the relatives of the 40 million victims of this expansion may have been less keen to call him a "hero." You could argue that seemingly half-crazed Colonel Gaddafi was a hero, wresting control of his country from foreign influence and rebuilding its entire infrastructure for the better, while you could also point out that the almost saintly Nelson Mandela's activism threatened the lives of innocent people. Adolf Hitler and Pol Pot may have conducted two of the worst genocides in history, slaughtering millions in their attempts to create their perverse visions of utopia, but what of Winston Churchill, often regarded as one of the greatest men of the twentieth century? He stood resolute against the might of the evil German Reich, but he also once suggested using chemical weapons to wipe out the Kurds in Mesopotamia, who were merely trying to protect their own land. If his memorandum had been acted upon, he too would have been responsible for genocide—it's sometimes a hair's breadth, a simple twist of fate, between heroism and villainy.

Some of the villains in this book are perhaps just unlucky—the evil reputations of Lucrezia Borgia and, to some extent, even the Emperor Caligula are born out of a haze of conjecture that has been built up in the absence of verifiable historical fact. Perhaps we should remember that in former times, history was almost always written by the victors or by the mouthpieces of new leaders who gained political capital by denigrating the reputations of those who had gone before. Also, historians from the West are likely to approach the facts with their own ideas of angels and demons, which may spur them on to paint a far different picture of the same events than a historian from the East, and vice versa.

Then there is the question of character. Many of the men and women described in this book share the same characteristics, whether they are hero or villain. Self-belief, determination, ruthlessness, perseverance, and a certainty of vision to overcome the odds, to score a victory, to make their dreams a reality—evidence of these personality traits fill the pages that follow, whether the subject is remembered with fondness or disgust. Whether they are deemed a hero or villain, their adventures, escapades, battles, and intrigues are littered with collateral damage.

Whichever side of the coin they fall on, or whether they alternate between the two depending on your perspective, they are like few other men and women. They were able to step beyond the bounds of the accepted world, for better or for worse, and have made their mark on history.

ANCIENT WORLD

History is littered with the legends and stories of heroes and villains, and the ancient world contributed a great number of characters who fill these roles. Alexander the Great's position in the pantheon of heroes is undiminished, as are the accomplishments of Hannibal. Legendary Roman leaders Julius Caesar, Caligula, and Nero, however, hold much more ambivalent positions in history, while Attila the Hun is seen as a villain from a Western perspective. He was, nevertheless, an outstanding military leader who conquered huge swathes of Roman-held Europe and contributed to the downfall of the Roman Empire.

Alexander the Great

SO OFTEN THE CHILDREN OF GREAT MEN ARE DAUNTED BY THEIR FATHERS AND
ARE DESTINED TO PLAY OUT A LIFE OF COMPARATIVE UNDERACHIEVEMENT IN THEIR
SHADOW, BUT ALEXANDER PROVED TO BE NO SUCH PROGENY.

His father, Philip II of Macedon, was a truly great man who took control of Greece, but his son was the one to earn the epithet "Great"—and to keep it, despite the revisions of history. He proved to be one of the greatest leaders, military strategists, and empirebuilders ever known, even though he died at the age of just 32.

When Alexander was born in 356 BC, the regions of southeastern Europe and the Middle East were in turmoil, with Persia and Athens as the dominant powers. The small kingdom of Macedon sat on the edge of the main affray to the north of Greece, across the Aegean Sea from the vast Persian empire. While Alexander was receiving an education from the philosopher Aristotle, his father Philip pushed his forces south to unite all Greece under his rule. By the time Alexander was 16, he began to lead troops into battle and soon proved his worth to his father. Then his whole world changed. Philip was assassinated in 336 BC and Alexander found himself, at 20, the head of a nation at war with its neighbors. The Greek states conquered by Philip revolted, so Alexander gathered his forces, headed south, and destroyed Thebes. Athens was in awe of his military acumen and aggression, and soon he established dominance over the Greek peninsula. He then took on the biggest challenge any leader could face—the Persian Empire, which controlled Egypt and all the lands of Asia Minor.

> *What Alexander lacked in manpower he gained in loyalty. His men were willing to die for their charismatic leader, who they knew would bear arms at their side.*

FACING THE PERSIAN EMPIRE

Alexander knew that his kingdom would never be safe unless he took the fight to the Persians, so in 334, he crossed the Dardanelles strait. At the Granicus river, he faced the world's greatest power in battle for the first time and won. A year later, he routed the leader of the Persians, Darius III, at Issus. While Darius licked his wounds, Alexander grasped Syria and made his mark on the continent of Africa, routing cities on his way to Egypt, where he was received with respect by the pharaoh.

DARIUS III PREPARES FOR BATTLE

Darius was not willing to see his power threatened by this young pup. If he could not defeat Alexander by strategy alone, he would use the sheer weight of numbers. In 331 BC, he amassed a huge army, possibly numbering 100,000 men, for the final great battle at Guagamela, on the banks of the Tigris river in Iraq. The Macedonian-led army had just 47,000 men, but what Alexander lacked in manpower he gained in loyalty. His men were willing to die for their charismatic leader, who they knew would bear arms at their side.

Darius, in contrast, was not even present at the Persians' defeat at Granicus, and fled the battle at Issus. Alexander outflanked and defeated the much larger Persian force, driving them into retreat.

ALEXANDER MARCHES ON

Following the victory, Alexander remained in the trading city of Babylon for a month before marching to Susa and Persepolis,

followed in 330 BC by Ecbatana in Iran. While there he learned the news he had been waiting for—Darius was dead. Yet his ambition did not falter. He swept east through Asia Minor, founding Macedonian colonies at Herat and Kandahar in Afghanistan. In 328 BC, he reached the plains of Sogdiana, where he married Roxana, the daughter of local nobleman Oxyartes. He pushed on to the Indus river in India and fought yet another ferocious battle, this time against Porus, a rajah of the Punjab, near the Hydaspes river. Alexander won once more, but this was the end of his trans-Asian escapade. His troops were exhausted, having conquered a vast swathe of the known world, and they lacked the resources and supply routes to push on any farther.

The undefeated Alexander led his army back along the Indus, reaching Susa in 324 BC, where he made a second, tactical marriage, to Darius' daughter. He moved on to his powerbase at Babylon, where, in June 323 BC, he died at the age of 32—not at the hand of a great Persian ruler, a king, or a rajah, but possibly the bite of a tiny mosquito, succumbing to what may have been a malarial fever. His huge new empire would soon falter and crumble, but the title of Alexander the Great would never wane.

Following page: The extent of Alexander's empire.

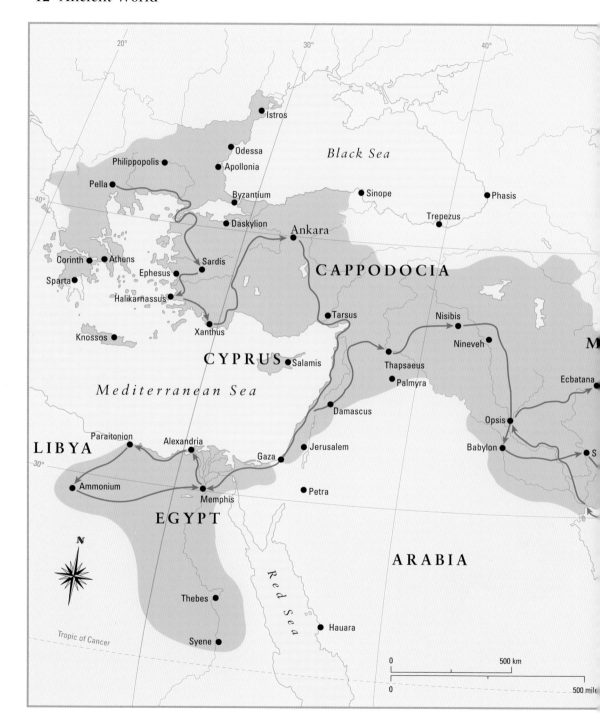

20° 30° 40°

Istros

Black Sea

Odessa
Philippopolis
Apollonia
Pella
Byzantium
Sinope
Phasis
Daskylion
Trepezus
Ankara

Corinth
Athens
Sardis
CAPPODOCIA
Ephesus
Sparta
Halikarnassus
Tarsus
Nisibis
Knossos
Xanthus
Nineveh

CYPRUS
Salamis
Thapsaeus
Palmyra
Ecbatana

Mediterranean Sea
Damascus
Opsis
Paraitonion
Alexandria
Babylon
LIBYA
Gaza
Jerusalem
Ammonium
Memphis
Petra
EGYPT

ARABIA

N

Red Sea

Thebes

Tropic of Cancer
Hauara
Syene

0 500 km

0 500 mile

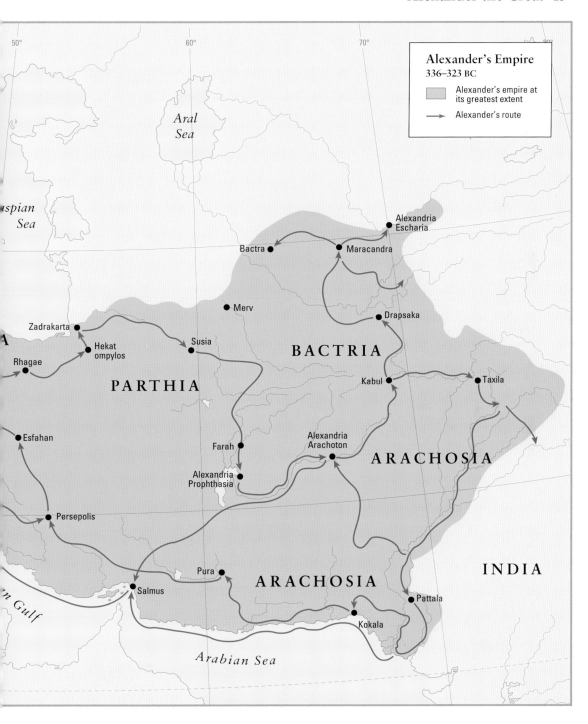

50°   60°   70°   80°

Aral
Sea

Alexander's Empire
336–323 BC

Alexander's empire at
its greatest extent

Alexander's route

Caspian
Sea

Alexandria
Escharia

Bactra   Maracandra

Merv

Drapsaka

BACTRIA

Zadrakarta

Hekat
ompylos   Susia

Rhagae

Taxila

Kabul

PARTHIA

Esfahan

Alexandria
Arachoton

Farah

ARACHOSIA

Alexandria
Prophthasia

Persepolis

INDIA

Pura

ARACHOSIA

Salmus
Pattala

Gulf

Kokala

Arabian Sea

Hannibal

IN THE THIRD CENTURY BC, ROME WAS ESTABLISHING A TERRITORIAL DOMINION THAT WOULD SWEEP ALL BEFORE IT AND LAST FOR **600** YEARS—BUT ONE MAN, A CARTHAGINIAN NAMED HANNIBAL, DECIDED TO STAND UP TO ROME'S AMBITIONS.

He would lead an assault that nearly extinguished the Roman Empire in its infancy, and conducted one of the most extraordinary military feats ever accomplished. Born in 247 BC, Hannibal was the son of Hamilcar Barca, a Carthaginian general. Even at the age of nine, Hannibal showed his warrior streak, imploring his father to let him join the campaign against the Romans in Spain. Hamilcar consented, but first made Hannibal swear eternal hatred of Rome, a promise he was to keep with a vengeance for the remainder of his years. Carthage, located in modern-day Tunisia, had much to fear from the Romans. It had built an empire along the African coast of the Mediterranean as well as controlling southern Spain, Corsica, Sardinia, and part of Sicily. Carthage was the commercial heart of the region and controlled much of the seafaring trade. The growing power and aggressive militancy of Rome put all this in jeopardy, leading to endless conflict. The course of the history of the Western world would depend on its outcome.

GENERAL OF THE CARTHAGINIAN ARMY

The Roman historian Livy described Hannibal's virtues in detail—from his bravery and stamina to his willingness to share the deprivations of his men—but also cataloged his shortcomings, including his cruelty. Hannibal never refrained from the most ruthless course of action, and gave little value to the sanctity of the lives of either friend and foe. As soon as he became general of the Carthaginian army in 221 BC at the age of 26, Hannibal decided that he would be the aggressor in the conflict with Rome.

He consolidated Carthaginian power in Spain, defeating local tribes before setting his army against the city of Saguntum, an ally of Rome. In 219 BC, he laid siege to the city for eight months before destroying it. It was a declaration of war, igniting the long Second Punic War with Rome. Hannibal was

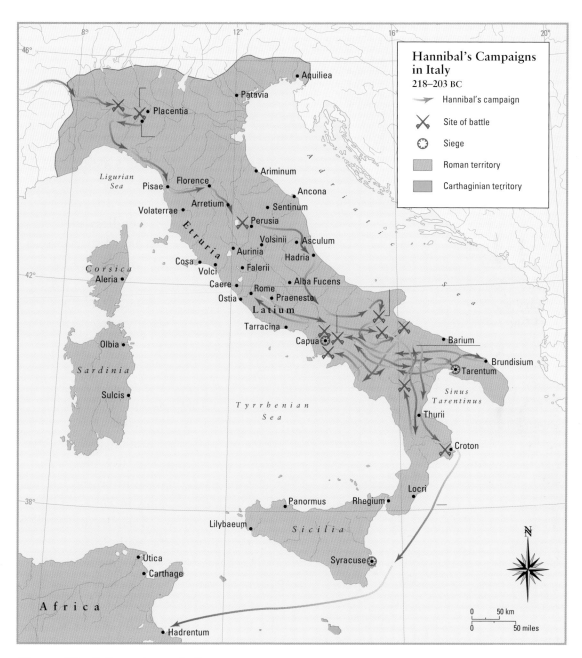

Hannibal's Campaigns in Italy
218–203 BC

→ Hannibal's campaign

⚔ Site of battle

◉ Siege

Roman territory

Carthaginian territory

The route of Hannibal's campaign over the Alps.

The ruins of Carthage—although Hannibal managed to take the fight to the Romans, they eventually laid waste to his city of Carthage.

not content to wait for the Romans to seek revenge in Spain; he believed that Carthage's security would only come if the city of Rome itself was defeated.

NO ORDINARY GENERAL

Hannibal knew that any assault by sea would be futile, because Rome had naval supremacy. Instead, he would attack by land, hoping to raise support from seditious northern Italian tribes that were disgruntled with Rome. The Romans never thought that an invading army would dare assault Rome by trying to march across the huge natural barrier of the Alps

in northern Italy, and especially not one coming from Spain, which would have to cross the Pyrenees first. But Hannibal was no ordinary general.

In 218, he fought his way through northern Spain, showing his aptitude for mountain warfare, and took an army of almost 40,000 foot soldiers, 8,000 cavalry, and 37 African elephants across the Pyrenees and toward the Alps. War elephants had been used before to charge into the heart of the enemy, crush foot soldiers, and cause mayhem, but no one had led a whole herd across such a perilous mountain region. In fact, the Alps proved perilous for Hannibal's men as well. Half his soldiers and all the elephants died in the torturous but successful attempt to cross the highest mountains in Europe.

THE BATTLE AT CANNAE

The use of elephants may be remembered as Hannibal's most unusual strategy, but it was his subtle craft on the field of war that marked him out as one of the great heroes of the era. He was an expert at outflanking his enemies, using a combination of infantry and cavalry to surround them. His army may have been depleted by the time he reached the Po Valley in northern Italy, but it was still large enough for Hannibal to put his military acumen to great use in an electrifying campaign. Rome had been completely outmaneuvered by his Alpine escapade. He took northern Italy before destroying Roman legions in a cunning ambush at Trasimene in 217 BC. A year later, the battle at Cannae would be the scene of Rome's greatest ever defeat. The huge Roman force of up to 100,000 men attempted to strike at the weak center of Hannibal's battle formation, but he simply surrounded it with his flanks and all but destroyed it.

FACED WITH CAPTURE

This eventually proved to be Hannibal's greatest battle, and his planned assault on the city of Rome never came to pass.

He managed to lead his troops to within three miles of the city walls in 211 BC, but his army was so depleted that he had to withdraw and await reinforcements from Carthage, which never arrived. Eventually, Hannibal had to return to Carthage in 203 to help defend it from a sustained Roman attack. The Romans finally defeated him in his own land in 202, but Hannibal remained a thorn in Rome's side for the next 20 years, as the Republic extended its influence over the whole region. Finally, faced with capture in ca. 182 BC, Hannibal took his own life.

FACT FILE

Hannibal

Born: 247 BC

Died: ca.182 BC

Birthplace: Carthage

Parents: Didobal and Hamilcar Barca

Historic Role: Military general and tactician for the Carthaginian army

Nemesis: The Roman Empire

Battles: Second Punic War (218–201 BC) Battles of Herdonia (210 BC and 212 BC), Trebia (218 BC), Lake Trasimene (217 BC), Cannae (216 BC), Zama (202 BC)

Hero or Villain: Carthaginian hero, but highly troublesome for Rome

Julius Caesar

JULIUS CAESAR WAS A GREAT MILITARY LEADER AND POLITICAL STRATEGIST, BUT HE WAS ALSO A COLD-BLOODED, POWER-HUNGRY KILLER. PERHAPS MORE THAN ANY OTHER HISTORICAL FIGURE, HE IS SEEN AS BOTH A HERO AND A VILLAIN.

Born Gaius Julius Caesar to a wealthy patrician family in 100 BC, he was able to prosper in the Roman Republic, advancing to junior elected offices before being appointed governor of Spain. He was a gifted orator who benefited hugely from the democratic system of the Republic, and seemed to be part of the establishment, but he was also a radical freethinker who had his eye on the main prize—complete control of Rome and its dominions. He struck up a strategic alliance with Crassus and Pompey, two high-profile politicians who had spent the previous decade at odds with each other. In 60 BC, they formed the First Triumvirate, effectively becoming joint heads of state. Caesar knew what he was doing—Crassus was probably the wealthiest man in Rome, while Pompey held great sway over the army, and Caesar thought he could control them within the Triumvirate.

During the First Triumvirate, Caesar used the time to match the wealth, military reputation, and popularity of the other two men. The Romans held in high regard the leaders of successful military campaigns, so Caesar immediately took a force to face the troublesome Gauls. He conquered the whole of Gaul and supposedly enslaved a million men, then in 52 BC, he remorselessly crushed a revolt by the Gallic leader Vercingetorix. During his governorship of Gaul, Caesar looked farther afield, bridging the Rhine to threaten the warring tribes of Germany and then crossing the English Channel twice, in 55 and 54 BC, to confront the mysterious tribes of Britain. He was forced to return to Gaul because of the threat of revolt, but he had made his mark as an adventurous leader.

A THREAT TO THE REPUBLIC

Caesar's relationship with Pompey was severely strained. Pompey realized that Caesar's increasing ambitions made him a threat to the whole Republic. After Crassus died, Rome was brought to the brink of civil war when Pompey and the

Senate demanded that Caesar disband his huge army and return to Rome. However, Julius saw the opportunity he had been waiting for. All he needed to do was get rid of Pompey who, like Julius himself, had gained huge popularity through his military exploits. Julius ignored the ruling of the Senate and convinced his army to fight Pompey, defeating him at Pharsalus in Greece in 48 BC. He then followed Pompey to Egypt to finish the job. There, Pompey was murdered by the boy-pharaoh's men to appease Caesar, who was presented with his severed head. Julius also had an affair with the pharaoh's sister Cleopatra, who bore him a son; he then defeated the pharaoh and installed her as his puppet ruler in Egypt.

A group of conspirators, including his friend Brutus, stabbed Caesar to death in the Senate, the bastion of Roman democracy. He died at the foot of a statue of Pompey.

VENI, VEDI, VICI

With the deaths of both Crassus and Pompey, the Roman political elite was in turmoil and granted Caesar the dictatorship of the Republic for one year. However, Julius knew that he could not rule the Roman populace by force alone. He needed its support if he was going to continue to be the absolute ruler, and his military dominance of foreign lands greatly appealed to Roman arrogance. Consequently, in 47 BC he pursued a stunning campaign against King Pharnaces II, who opposed Roman control of Asia Minor. After his devastating victory, Caesar uttered the immortal line "*Veni vidi vici*" ("I came, I saw, I conquered"). On his return to Rome, he was awarded a ten-year dictatorship by the Roman political hierarchy acting out of respect, awe, and fear of this man who seemed to be able to quash his enemies at will. However, Caesar still felt insecure and headed back to Africa to defeat Republican Cato, slaughtering his army instead of accepting its surrender. Caesar returned to Spain to defeat the sons of Pompey at Munda in 45 BC. With all opposition to his absolute rule destroyed, in 46 BC Caesar accepted a dictatorship for life. On that day, the Roman Republic, founded on the democratic principles of Ancient Greece, was extinguished and the Roman Empire was born. However, Caesar failed to see the dangers close to home. On March 15, 44 BC (the Ides of March), a group of conspirators, including Brutus, stabbed Caesar to death in the Senate House, the bastion of Roman democracy. He died at the foot of a statue of Pompey.

The extent of the Roman Empire (overleaf) in 55 BC.

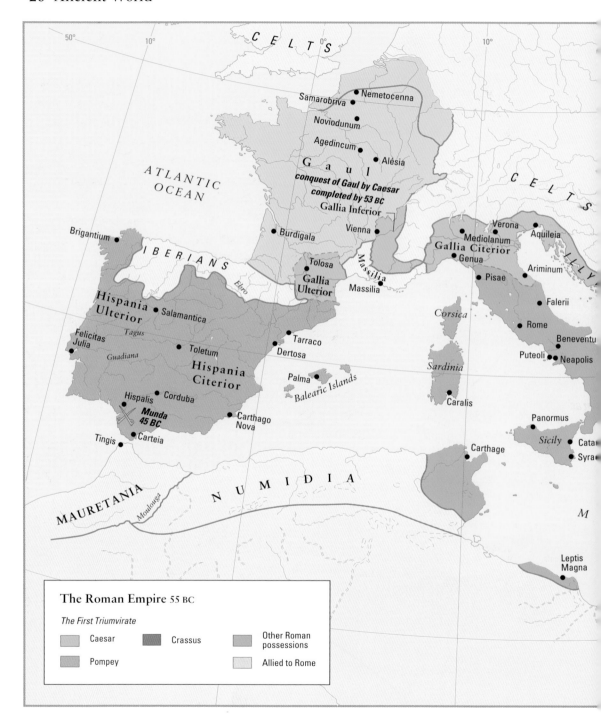

50° 10° 10°

C E L T S

● Nemetocenna
Samarobriva ●
Noviodunum ●
Agedincum ●
● Alésia

G a u l
conquest of Gaul by Caesar
completed by 53 BC
Gallia Inferior

Vienna

C E L T S

ATLANTIC
OCEAN

Verona ●
Mediolanum ● ● Aquileia
Gallia Citerior
Genua ●

I L L Y

Brigantium ●

I B E R I A N S

● Burdigala

Massilia

Ariminum ●

Tolosa ●
Gallia
Ulterior
Massilia

Pisae ●

● Falerii

Ebro

● Rome

Corsica

Hispania
Ulterior ● Salamantica

Tagus

Tarraco ●
Dertosa

● Beneventu
Puteoli ● ● Neapolis

Felicitas
Julia

Guadiana

● Toletum

Hispania
Citerior

Sardinia

Palma ●
Balearic Islands

Hispalis ● Corduba

Munda
45 BC

● Carthago
Nova

Caralis ●

Panormus ●

Tingis ● ● Carteia

Sicily ● Cata
● Syra

Carthage ●

M A U R E T A N I A

Moulouga

N U M I D I A

M

Leptis
Magna

The Roman Empire 55 BC

The First Triumvirate

Caesar

Crassus

Other Roman
possessions

Pompey

Allied to Rome

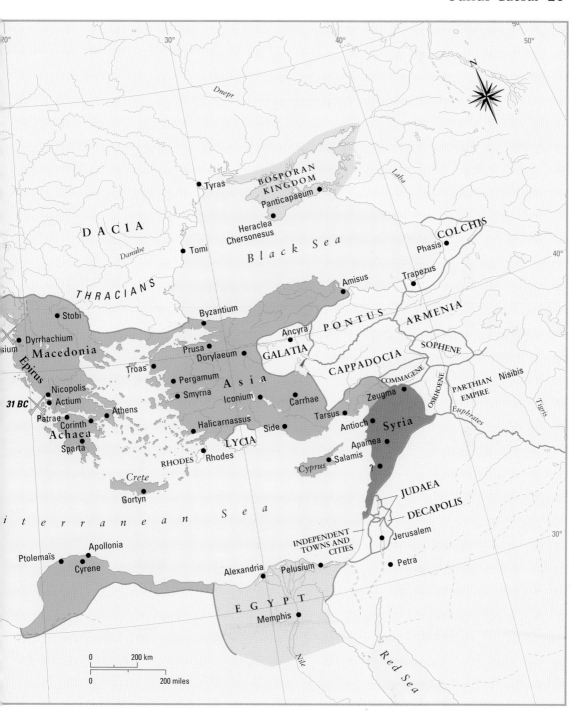

20°   30°   40°   50°

Dnepr

DACIA

Danube

BOSPORAN
KINGDOM
• Panticapaeum

• Tyras

Heraclea
Chersonesus

COLCHIS

• Phasis

40°

• Tomi

Black Sea

Amisus •

Trapezus •

THRACIANS

• Stobi

Byzantium

PONTUS   ARMENIA

Ancyra •

Dyrrhachium •

Macedonia

Prusa •
Dorylaeum •

GALATIA

SOPHENE

...ium ×

Epirus

Troas •

CAPPADOCIA

COMMAGENE

Nisibis

• Nicopolis

Pergamum •

Asia

PARTHIAN
EMPIRE

Tigris

31 BC ×

• Actium

• Smyrna

Iconium •

Carrhae •

Zeugma •

ORRHOENE

Euphrates

Patrae •

Athens •

Tarsus •

Syria

Corinth •

Halicarnassus •

Side •

Antioch •

Achaea

Sparta •

LYCIA

Apamea •

RHODES • Rhodes

Cyprus • Salamis

?

Crete

JUDAEA

• Gortyn

DECAPOLIS

i t e r r a n e a n   S e a

INDEPENDENT
TOWNS AND
CITIES

Jerusalem •

30°

Apollonia •

Petra •

Ptolemaïs •

• Cyrene

Alexandria •   Pelusium •

E G Y P T

Memphis •

Nile

Red Sea

0   200 km

0   200 miles

Caligula

IN FOLKLORE, CALIGULA IS AN INSANE, MURDEROUS TYRANT WHO WAS SUCH A CRACKPOT THAT HE WANTED TO GIVE HIS FAVORITE HORSE A POSITION OF POWER. IN FACT, VERY LITTLE ABOUT HIS RULE AS ROMAN EMPEROR HAS BEEN PROVEN.

Born August 31, AD 12, Gaius Julius Caesar Augustus Germanicus was the third child of Germanicus, a popular and successful general who was the nephew and adopted son of Emperor Tiberius. The young boy soon earned the nickname "Caligula," meaning "little soldier's boot," because he wore a miniature uniform while accompanying his father on his campaigns in Germany. After the death of Germanicus in AD 19, Caligula's mother Agrippina, unwisely provoked Tiberius to the extent that most of Caligula's siblings were caught in the fallout and died in exile or prison. By contrast, Caligula, deemed to be something of a sycophantic actor when it came to his dealings with the emperor, inveigled himself to such an extent that he became Tiberius' joint heir with his cousin Tiberius Gemellus.

Emperor Tiberius died in 37, with some Roman historians claiming that Caligula or his friend Macro, a Praetorian Prefect, hastened his journey toward the Styx river with the aid of a suffocating pillow. As Tiberius was 77, there is little reason to doubt the contemporary historian Philo's view that he died of natural causes, but Caligula's later actions give some credibility to the rumor of murder. He was a power-hungry young man, and quickly managed to have Gemellus excised from Tiberius' will so that he could become sole emperor.

THE GOLDEN DAYS

Surprisingly, Caligula's initial reign was something of a golden period. As the son of the fondly remembered Germanicus, and as an alternative to the tyrannical Tiberius, his rise to power was met with public rejoicing. He arranged public games, improved the lot of the military, restored democratic elections, lowered taxation, and abandoned Tiberius' most unreasonable policies. However, he was also wary of his rivals and had some members of his own family, including Tiberius Gemellus, executed or exiled. Macro also knew too

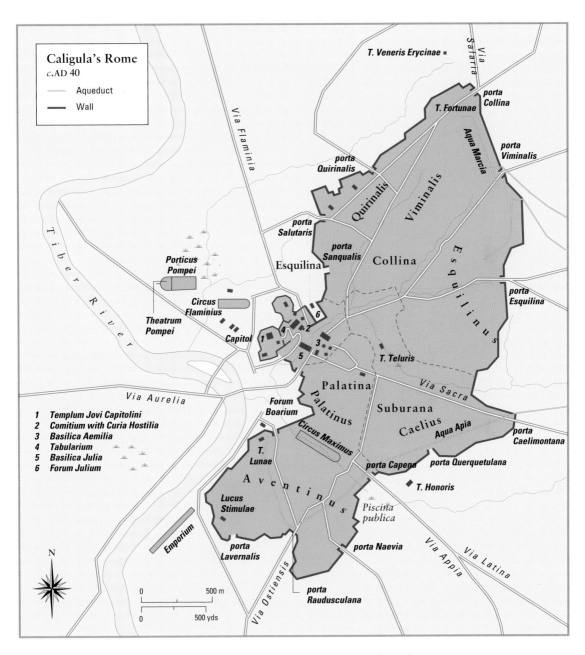

Caligula's Rome
*c.*AD 40

— Aqueduct
━ Wall

T. Veneris Erycinae ■

Via Salaria

porta Collina

T. Fortunae

Aqua Marcia

porta Viminalis

porta Quirinalis

Via Flaminia

Quirinalis

Viminalis

porta Salutaris

porta Sanqualis

Collina

Esquilina

Esquilinus

porta Esquilina

Porticus Pompei

Tiber River

Circus Flaminius

Theatrum Pompei

Capitol

6

4

7

2

3

5

T. Teluris

Via Sacra

Via Aurelia

Forum Boarium

Palatina

Palatinus

Suburana

Caelius

Aqua Apia

porta Caelimontana

1 Templum Jovi Capitolini
2 Comitium with Curia Hostilia
3 Basilica Aemilia
4 Tabularium
5 Basilica Julia
6 Forum Julium

Circus Maximus

porta Capena

porta Querquetulana

T. Lunae

T. Honoris

A v e n t i n u s

Piscina publica

Lucus Stimulae

Emporium

porta Lavernalis

porta Naevia

Via Ostiensis

Via Appia

Via Latina

porta Radusculana

N

0   500 m

0   500 yds

The city of Rome as it was in Caligula's reign.

This bust of Caligula gives no hint of his later madness.

accusations against wealthy citizens, sequestering their property without a proper trial. To raise further funds, he introduced new taxes and penalties that were even worse than those of Tiberius. Part of his fortune was spent on his own imperial palace complex, but he was also responsible for a great program of public works, completing a major theater, temple, and racetrack, as well the construction of two aqueducts. He also had a giant obelisk transported from Egypt to Rome, where it still stands today as the Vatican Obelisk.

STRANGE TIMES

This was not enough to appease the Senate, which felt increasingly insulted by Caligula's strange behaviou=r. He made his sister Julia Drusilla the imperial heir and, when she died in AD 38, he forced the senators to deify her as a goddess. He put some senators on trial for treason and had them put to death. Consequently, various conspiracies against him were already emerging by AD 39, just two years into his reign. Caligula is believed to have started referring to himself as a god, and replaced heads on statues of deities with his own image. His attempts at self-deification also gave rise to problems in the Roman provinces—there were riots in Alexandria when statues of him were erected in Jewish synagogues, and his order to have a

much for his own good and was forced to commit suicide. Yet this could be considered as little more than par for the course for a Roman emperor.

MATTERS OF MIND AND MONEY

Caligula's descent into more peculiar and vengeful behavior may have been spurred on by an illness that altered the stability of his mind. In any case, his popularity began to wane. He laid waste to Tiberius' vast fortune and then began to make statue of himself placed in the Temple of Jerusalem threatened war in the region.

THE SENATE VERSUS THE PUBLIC

The historian Suetonius, writing in the second century AD, is responsible for some of the wilder tales of Caligula's rule. Given that he was writing some hundred years after the fact, Suetonius' comments need to be taken with a pinch of salt. Caligula is alleged to have had sex with his own sisters and sold their services to other men, to have raped and killed on a whim, and to have made his horse Incitatus a priest before planning to make it into a consul. Whatever the reality, he had become unpopular with the ruling elite in a short space of time; members of the Praetorian Guard, seemingly with the consent of senior senators and the army, stabbed him to death on January 24, AD 41. However, the public rejected the Senate's desire to return to the days of the Republic, preferring to allow Caligula's supposedly half-witted brother Claudius to take power.

> *Part of his fortune was spent on his own imperial palace complex, but he was also responsible for a great program of public works.*

FACT FILE

Caligula

Born: August 31, AD 12

Died: January 24, AD 41

Birthplace: Antium, Italy

Nationality: Ancient Roman

Parents: Germanicus Julius Caesar (15 BC–AD 19) and Agrippina the Elder (ca.14 BC–AD 33)

Historic Role: Roman Emperor

Reign: AD 37–41

Marital Alliances: Junia Claudilla (33–34), Livia Orestilla (ca. 37), Lollia Paulina (38), Milonia Caesonia (38–41)

Historic Feats: In the early years, Caligula abandoned Tiberius' most unreasonable policies. Later on, he built an imperial palace and a great program of public works.

Hero or Villain: Caligula's coronation was met with public celebration, but his reign was tainted by villainy.

Nero

THE EMPEROR NERO IS ALLEGED TO HAVE SET FIRE TO
HIS OWN CITY AND THEN PLAYED HIS FIDDLE WHILE THE
CITY OF ROME BURNT, A PHRASE THAT HAS PASSED INTO
THE ENGLISH LANGUAGE TO DESCRIBE THE NEGLECT OF
PRIORITIES DURING A CRISIS.

Lucius Domitius Ahenobarbus, later nicknamed Nero,
was born into a distinguished family in AD 37. He can be
blamed for a number of things, from the murder of his
mother and wife to the persecution of early Christians, but the
fiddling while Rome burnt cannot be authenticated. His mother
was the power-hungry, manipulative Julia Agrippina, the sister of
Caligula. After the death of Nero's father, Agrippina married the
Roman emperor Claudius, who was her own uncle, got him to
adopt Nero as his heir, and encouraged Nero to marry Claudius'
daughter Octavia, who was both his adoptive sister and his cousin.
Not content with merely paving the way for her favored son to
become heir to the empire, she also removed the final hurdle when
she murdered Claudius himself in AD 54.

POETRY AND DEBAUCHERY

When Nero came to power at the age of just 16, he was an
aspiring poet and connoisseur of the arts who enjoyed performing
in public. The first years of his rule were restrained, especially
because he often took the advice of the philosopher Seneca
above that of his mother. However, in AD 55, he almost certainly
poisoned Claudius' son Britannicus, to make sure that there was

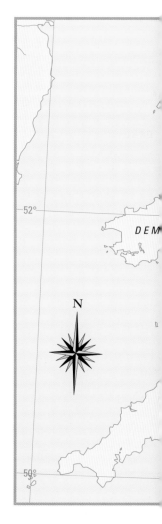

During Nero's reign, Boudicca led a revolt in what is now Britain against the Roman occupation.

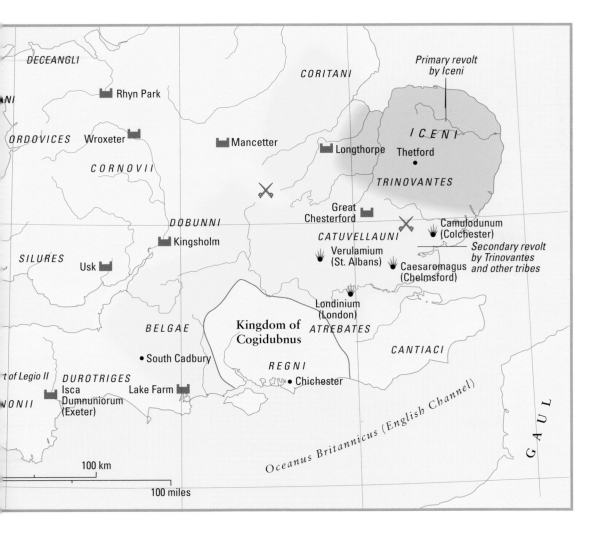

Boudiccan Revolts ca. AD 60–61

Primary area of revolt

Secondary area of revolt

Town attacked by rebels

Major battles

Fortresses of legions

Civilian site

DECEANGLI

Rhyn Park

CORITANI

Primary revolt
by Iceni

ORDOVICES   Wroxeter

Mancetter

ICENI

CORNOVII

Longthorpe   Thetford

TRINOVANTES

DOBUNNI

Great
Chesterford

Camulodunum
(Colchester)

Kingsholm

CATUVELLAUNI

Secondary revolt
by Trinovantes
and other tribes

SILURES

Usk

Verulamium
(St. Albans)

Caesaromagus
(Chelmsford)

Londinium
(London)

BELGAE

Kingdom of
Cogidubnus

ATREBATES

South Cadbury

CANTIACI

REGNI

t of Legio II   DUROTRIGES

Chichester

ONII   Isca
Dumnuniorum
(Exeter)

Lake Farm

Oceanus Britannicus (English Channel)

GAUL

100 km

100 miles

no imperial rival, while his love of life soon veered into a level of debauchery that shocked even the wilder factions of Roman society. It is thought that he took his own mother as his lover. Wracked with guilt and weary of her influence, he had her killed in AD 59, followed three years later by her disciple Octavia, who Nero had the nerve to accuse of adultery on a trumped-up charge. By this time, the role of Seneca, his restraining influence, had been diminished and Nero allowed his worst excesses to rule how he made decisions. Despite this, some of Nero's foreign policies met with success, with a campaign against the Parthian Empire in AD 58–63 and the incorporation of the Bosporan kingdom into the Roman Empire in AD 63. In newly conquered Britain, Queen Boudicca of the Iceni led a revolt in AD 61 that destroyed Camulodunum (Colchester), and then burned London and St. Albans to the ground at the cost of perhaps 100,000 lives. The revolt was eventually put down by the Roman governor Suetonius Paulinus in the West Midlands.

In AD 65, mounting dissatisfaction with Nero's excesses led to an assassination plot headed by the pro-Republican statesman Gaius Calpurnius Piso.

GREAT FIRE

One of the major events of Nero's reign was the Great Fire of Rome in AD 64. The claim of fiddling while Rome was burning largely comes from the sensationalist historian Suetonius, who wrote in the early second century that Nero set fire to the city and climbed to the top of the Tower of Maecenas. From that vantage point, he is said to have happily played an instrument (perhaps a lyre) and sang as the blaze caught hold and destroyed much of Rome. There's little doubt that the tale is apocryphal—when the fire started, Nero was not even in Rome, but 30 miles (50 km) away in Antium. However, the fire did fuel both the most acclaimed and derided episodes in Nero's life.

REBUILDING AND RELIGIOUS ZEAL

Razing the city allowed him to clear the slums and conduct an immense series of public works that stand as a testament to his better, public spirited attributes. Meanwhile, he helped to administer a huge relief effort for the many thousands of newly homeless people. He also took the opportunity to build the huge, architecturally adventurous palace complex of the *Domus Aurea* (the Golden House) for himself. The Domus covered an area of a third of a square mile (1 km square) and featured 300 rooms decorated with white

Nero undertook a series of building projects in Rome, some to improve the infrastructure of the city.

marble and frescoes. On the other hand he was able to use the fire as an excuse to vent his hatred for Christians, then a minor religious sect, whom he blamed for starting the blaze. He persecuted them, having them fed to dogs or nailed to crosses, and he is even said to have burnt Christians in order to light his garden at night according to the historian Tacitus.

RETALIATION AND REBELLION

In AD 65, mounting dissatisfaction with Nero's excesses led to an assassination plot headed by the pro-Republican statesman Gaius Calpurnius Piso. The plot was foiled, and Nero retaliated with a purge that involved the execution of many leading Romans, including Seneca. He was also said to have kicked to death his second wife. There was discontent throughout the empire and the governors of both Spain and Gaul rebelled against him, along with the all-important Praetorian Guard in Rome. Nero knew his days were numbered and fled Rome; the Senate declared him a public enemy and intended to have him beaten to death. Nero took his own life on June 9, AD 68, the anniversary of Octavia's death.

Attila the Hun

BY THE FIFTH CENTURY, THE NOW-CHRISTIAN ROMAN EMPIRE HAD BEEN DIVIDED INTO EASTERN AND WESTERN HALVES, AND THE POWER OF THE WEST WAS GREATLY DIMINISHED. THE DIVIDED EMPIRE FACED AN ONSLAUGHT BY A RAMPAGING BARBARIAN KING WHO THOUGHT HE COULD BRING ALL EUROPE TO ITS KNEES.

Attila may be commonly known by the epithet "the Hun," but he was also known by the more menacing "Scourge of God." The latter title more accurately reflects the awe and fear felt in Europe during the time when he even threatened Rome. He was born ca. 406 and became joint king of the Huns with his brother Bleda in AD 434.

The nomadic Huns, a fierce fighting race who were feared for their use of mounted archers and javelins, had migrated westward from Asia to control a region that stretched eastward from the Alps to the Caspian Sea. The Eastern Roman Empire, continually threatened by the warmongering Huns, was already paying them a tribute in order to keep the peace, but failed to keep up the payments. Attila knew that the whole Empire was weakening and that intimidation and bullying, instead of diplomacy, would be the key to his success. The Huns attacked the Eastern Empire in 441 and 443, assaulting cities along the Danube river, which was all important for trade in the region. The imperial forces were defeated at Gallipoli, and were forced to pay both a huge fine for reneging on previous payments and a much larger annual tribute.

Returning to his kingdom, Attila did not want to share the spoils with his brother, so he murdered him in 445. With domestic matters sorted, he returned to attack the Eastern Empire in 447–449, invading the Balkan territories and laying waste to much of Greece. Constantinople, the capital of the Eastern Empire, was only just saved from destruction, but hundreds of towns were taken, and many thousands slaughtered, including innumerable nuns and priests. In the resulting peace treaty, Attila again exhorted heavy damages from the Eastern Empire in tributes and fines.

The strategy that sealed Attila the Hun's fate.

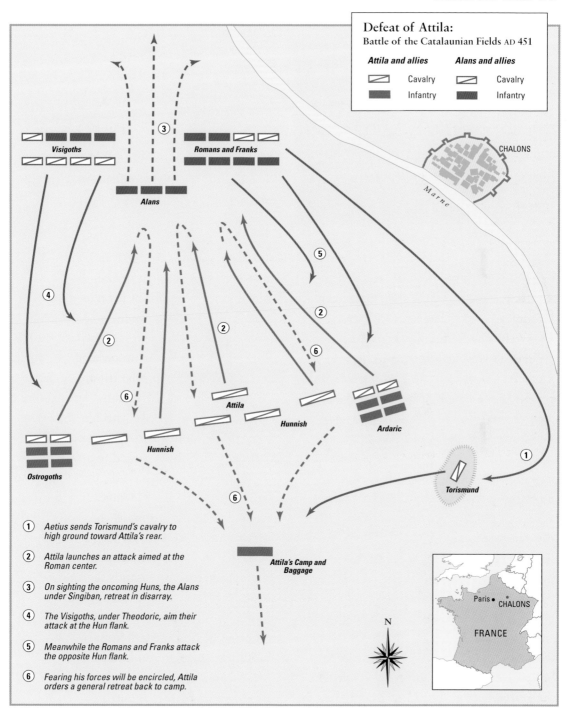

Defeat of Attila:
Battle of the Catalaunian Fields AD 451

Attila and allies		*Alans and allies*	
▱	Cavalry	▱	Cavalry
▪	Infantry	▪	Infantry

CHALONS

Marne

Visigoths

Romans and Franks

③

Alans

⑤

④

②

②

②

⑥

Attila

Hunnish

⑥

Ardaric

Hunnish

Ostrogoths

⑥

Torismund

①

⑥

Attila's Camp and
Baggage

N

① Aetius sends Torismund's cavalry to
high ground toward Attila's rear.

② Attila launches an attack aimed at the
Roman center.

③ On sighting the oncoming Huns, the Alans
under Singiban, retreat in disarray.

④ The Visigoths, under Theodoric, aim their
attack at the Hun flank.

⑤ Meanwhile the Romans and Franks attack
the opposite Hun flank.

⑥ Fearing his forces will be encircled, Attila
orders a general retreat back to camp.

Paris • CHALONS

FRANCE

Mór Than's painting of The Feast of Attila.

EYES ON A BIGGER PRIZE

However, Attila thought that there was a bigger prize available—the Western Empire, which included the traditional powerbases of Rome and Gaul. In 450, Honoria, the sister of Valentinian III (Emperor of the Western Empire), was being forced into an arranged marriage by her brother. She appealed to Attila for assistance, sending her engagement ring with the message. Hardly a gallant knight who felt honor-bound to save a damsel in distress, Attila nonetheless saw his opportunity to attack and, perhaps deliberately mistaking the ring for a promise of marriage, demanded half the Western Empire as a dowry.

His forces ransacked cities, slaughtering soldiers and clergy alike, before reaching Orléans in Gaul in 451. There, they came up against the combined strategic capabilities and ruthlessness of the Roman general Flavius Aetius, and Theodoric, king of the Visigoths, a tribe that was just as fierce as the Huns and had long been a thorn in the side of the Empire before briefly becoming its ally. Attila had just successfully besieged Orléans when they arrived, but realized that he, too, would be besieged if he held onto the city, and so sought more advantageous terrain.

THE LAST GREAT VICTORY

During the Battle of the Catalaunian Fields, the Huns made a cataclysmic attempt to take the center of a high ridge from which they could dictate the battlefield, but the Roman allies repulsed them and sent them fleeing in disarray, injuring Attila in the process. The allies could have slaughtered the remaining Huns in their entirety, but withdrew on the news of Theodoric's death. It was the last great victory for the Western Roman Empire.

THE MASTER OF ALL EUROPE?

The defeated but unbowed Attila was still intent on proving that he was the master of all Europe, and continued to demand Honoria's hand. In 452, he regrouped and drove into Italy, threatening Rome and Pope Leo I himself. He rampaged through the cities of the north and razed Aquileia so it simply ceased to exist. He was known as *Flagellum Dei* (the Scourge of God), because many felt that the terror he was

Renaissance medal with the legend, "Atila, Flagelum Dei."

able to launch on Christianity was divine retribution for the waywardness of the Church. However, his depredations were curtailed by famine and disease.

Having finally given up the prospect of marrying Honoria, Attila married Ildico in 453, but this proved to be his undoing. He died on his wedding night, either by the hand of his new bride or from a hemorrhage brought on by heavy drinking and feasting. The Western Empire breathed a sigh of relief, but its frailties had been exposed. By 476, just 24 years later, it had completely collapsed and Rome itself was controlled by barbarians from the north.

FACT FILE

Attila the Hun

Born: ca. AD 406

Died: AD 453

Race: The Huns

Historic Role: King of the Huns and leader of the Hunnic Empire (434–453)

Marital Alliances: Ildico (453)

Battles and Sieges: Invasion of the Eastern Roman Empire (441 and 447); Invasion of the Western Roman Empire (451–452); Battle of the Catalaunian Fields (451)

Historic Feats: Became known as *Flagellum Dei* (the Scourge of God) and exposed the frailties of the Roman Empire

Circumstances of Death: Hemorrhage in suspicious circumstances

Hero or Villain: A Hunnic hero, but highly troublesome for Rome

MIDDLE AGES

A period full of event, bloodshed, and battle, the Middle Ages gave rise to many well-known and notorious characters. Saladin and Richard the Lionheart fought against each other in the great crusades, but both emerge as heroic figures. The reputation of Genghis Khan is a harder call, because there is no doubt that he was a powerful albeit violent conqueror. Both Robert the Bruce and Owain Glyndwr fought campaigns of independence for their respective countries, and Joan of Arc helped rally the French crown against the English occupation. All three emerge as heroes, while Tomás de Torquemada is remembered as the villainous father of the Inquisition. Vlad the Impaler has earned a similar place in history, while the notoriety of early Renaissance beauty Lucrezia Borgia may have been largely based on propaganda and the failings of her murderous family.

Saladin

THE TWELFTH-CENTURY MUSLIM CONQUEROR OF JERUSALEM WHO REPULSED THE THIRD CRUSADE, SALADIN MAY HAVE BEEN A VILLAIN TO SOME PEOPLE, BUT HE REMAINS ONE OF THE GREATEST HEROES IN THE HISTORY OF THE MIDDLE EAST.

The Kurd Selah'edînê Eyubî (al ad-D n Y suf ibn Ayy b in Arabic), was born in Tikrit (Iraq) ca. 1138, but he came to be known by the simplified name of Saladin in the West. He was a very religious young man, but in time he would found the Ayyubid dynasty on his exploits as an extraordinary military strategist. His military studies were aided by his uncle, Asad al-din Shirkuh, a commander in the Zengid dynasty, which had scored notable victories against early Frankish Crusaders in the Middle East.

The Crusades, which began in 1095 with the support of the pope, were given the mission to secure the Holy Land in the Middle East, and involved Franks, Italians, and, later, English noblemen. Their most notable victory was the Siege of Jerusalem, in which they defeated a combined Jewish and Muslim force to take the city in 1099, and they managed to set up a Crusader kingdom between Syria and Egypt.

Saladin soon put his uncle's training to good use, helping him to take over Egypt on behalf of Nur ad-Din, the head of the Zengid dynasty. Over the course of ten years, from 1164–74, Saladin grew in importance, taking the reins of power in Egypt from the Fatimid dynasty and reinstating the Sunni Islam faith in what had been a Shi-ite area. He also became involved in campaigns against the Frankish Crusaders, and annexed Yemen to form part of his burgeoning new empire. He paid off Nur ad-Din for his initial involvement in the conquest of Egypt and took the title "Sultan of Egypt." However, he could not rest on his laurels. With the death of Nur ad-Din in 1174, Syria, and its all-important ancient capital of Damascus, was a sitting target for the Crusaders. Instead of securing it by force, Saladin nervously waited for an invitation to come to Syria's aid while other interested parties began to make threats against the

The extent of Saladin's empire in the twelfth century.

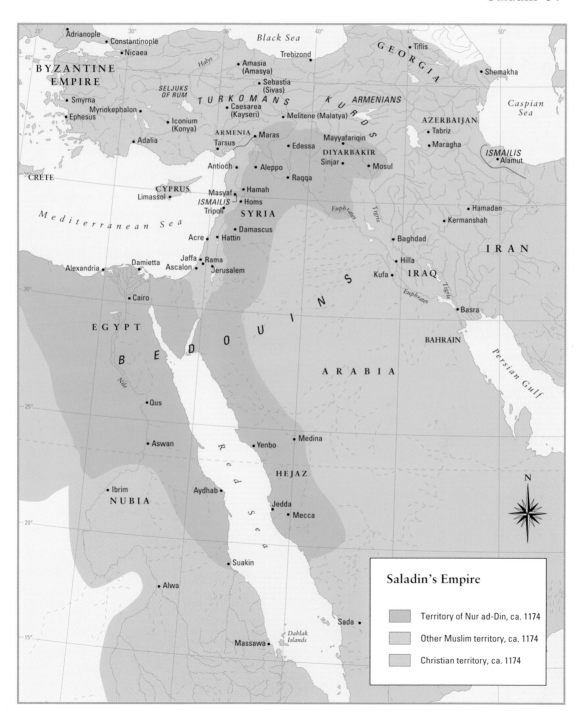

Adrianople
Constantinople
Nicaea
Black Sea
GEORGIA
Tiflis
Shemakha
BYZANTINE
EMPIRE
Halys
Amasia
(Amasya)
Trebizond
SELJUKS
OF RUM
TURKOMANS
Sebastia
(Sivas)
KURDS
ARMENIANS
Caspian
Sea
Smyrna
Myriokephalon
Ephesus
Caesarea
(Kayseri)
Melitene (Malatya)
AZERBAIJAN
Tabriz
Iconium
(Konya)
ARMENIA
Tarsus
Maras
Edessa
Mayyafariqin
DIYARBAKIR
Maragha
Adalia
ISMAILIS
Alamut
CRETE
Antioch
Aleppo
Sinjar
Mosul
CYPRUS
Masyaf
Hamah
Raqqa
Limassol
ISMAILIS
Tripoli
Homs
SYRIA
Euphrates
Tigris
Hamadan
Kermanshah
Mediterranean Sea
Acre
Hattin
Damascus
Baghdad
IRAN
Jaffa
Rama
Hilla
Alexandria
Damietta
Ascalon
Jerusalem
Kufa
IRAQ
Euphrates
Tigris
Cairo
B E D O U I N S
Basra
EGYPT
BAHRAIN
B
Nile
ARABIA
Persian Gulf
Qus
Aswan
Yenbo
Medina
Red Sea
HEJAZ
N
Ibrim
NUBIA
Aydhab
Jedda
Mecca
Suakin
Alwa
Sada
Dahlak
Islands
Massawa

Saladin's Empire

Territory of Nur ad-Din, ca. 1174

Other Muslim territory, ca. 1174

Christian territory, ca. 1174

region. Eventually, the emir of Damascus appealed to Saladin, who raced to the city with 700 horsemen.

RECOVERING JERUSALEM

Having secured Damascus, Saladin set about adding more of Nur ad-Din's former empire to his portfolio; by 1187, he had united Egypt, Syria, Palestine, Yemen, and northern Mesopotamia with the aim of protecting the entire region from the Frankish Crusaders. In that year, as a result of the Battle of Hattin on June 4, he finally recovered the Kingdom of Jerusalem from Christian control, which had endured for 88 years. The Crusader army was led by Guy of Lusignan (King of Jerusalem) and Raymond III of Tripoli, and Saladin knew that he could never overcome their defenses at their base in Tzippori. Saladin set a trap for Guy by using just a small part of his army to attack and capture Raymond's castle of Tiberias. Despite protestations from Raymond that it was a ploy, Guy took the bait and was lured into a field battle. Saladin cut off his army's line of retreat and carefully surrounded it—the outcome was inevitable.

The Christian conquest of Jerusalem had been a bloody affair, notable for the Crusaders' penchant for mass slaughter. In contrast, Saladin treated the inhabitants with respect, and demanded that the behavior of his troops remain courteous and civilized to innocent civilians.

PEACE WITH RICHARD THE LIONHEART

The capture of Jerusalem brought about the unlikely alliance of Philip II of France and Richard I of England, who mounted the Third Crusade in 1189. Richard I of England himself traversed Europe to defend the faith from what he saw as an infidel invader. The Third Crusade turned into a long war of attrition, because Saladin simply could not be mastered. Following the stalemate, Saladin finally made peace with Richard in 1192. Richard was able to return to Europe without disgrace, but, in fact, the only land ceded to the Crusaders in the peace treaty was a little strip from Tyre to Jaffa. Saladin died from a fever in the following year, but the city of Jerusalem remained in Muslim hands until the twentieth century.

A LEARNED CIVILIZED MAN

What Richard found in his dealings with Saladin was entirely unexpected. Here was a learned, civilized leader of men, who treated his captives with honor and caused no more bloodshed than he thought necessary. He was far removed from the evil barbarian of the Western imagination. Many of the most acclaimed heroic leaders in history have an egomaniacal streak that allows them to expend the lives of others in the pursuit of their own goals, but it appears that Saladin remained noble, virtuous, and pious while acting as a major player on the world stage. Richard I became an admirer, and Saladin's reputation for chivalry extended throughout Europe.

FACT FILE

Saladin

Born: ca. 1138

Died: 1193

Birthplace: Tikrit, Iraq

Nationality: Kurd

Religion: Islam

Historic Role: Sultan of Egypt, Syria, Palestine, and Yemen; Conqueror of Jerusalem

Historic Feats: The union of Egypt, Syria, Palestine, Yemen, and Northern Mesopotamia; the capture of Jerusalem

Legacy: Jerusalem remained in Muslim hands until the twentieth century

Hero or Villain: Hero

Richard the Lionheart

RICHARD I IS ONE OF THE MOST HERALDED KINGS OF ENGLAND. HE APPEARED TO BE THE EPITOME OF THE FINER CHARACTERISTICS OF ENGLISHNESS, SHOWING FORTITUDE, FAITH, BRAVERY, AND MORAL STRENGTH IN TIMES OF GREAT DIFFICULTY; YET THAT'S ONLY ONE PERSPECTIVE.

Another view would regard him as an absent monarch with greater concern abroad than at home. He rarely set foot in England, and when he did, he complained about the weather. He preferred Aquitaine and could not speak English at all.

Born in 1157, Richard was the third son of Henry II, who ruled England, Brittany, and Aquitaine. He rebelled against his father—unsuccessfully—when he was just 16. However, he proved an adept military leader, securing the territory of Aquitaine against rival claimants. Following the deaths of his elder brothers, he became Henry II's heir to the throne of England, but Henry insisted that his youngest son, John, should be given Aquitaine. Consequently, Richard joined forces with Philip II of France, defeating Henry's army at Ballans in southwestern France in July 1189. Henry died two days later and Richard became king of England. Richard's coronation was marred by anti-Semitic violence inspired by his decision to bar all Jews from his court, but he had a different religious persecution in mind—the Muslims in the Holy Land.

The Third Crusade was ignited by Saladin's capture of Jerusalem from prior Frankish Crusaders in 1187. The Christian kings of the West thought it their duty to reclaim the Holy City from Muslim hands, so Philip II of France and Richard I joined forces again to attack Saladin. Richard spent just six months of his reign in England, in which he is reported to have complained about the rain, and spent most of his time raising money from taxes for the campaign, declaring that he would have sold London if he had found a buyer. In 1190, he and Philip left for the Middle East, with 8,000 men and 100 ships.

MILITARY STRATEGIST

Richard's military abilities soon came to the fore when he conquered the island of Cyprus in the course of the journey. This was an important logistical maneuver, because it helped the Crusaders control routes to the Middle East through the Mediterranean. He landed at Acre, north of Jerusalem, in June 1191 and, despite suffering from scurvy, he helped to capture the city of Acre from Saladin. Philip II, who was also ill, then returned home, leaving Richard to conclude the Crusade with the capture of Jerusalem. He took his forces south toward the city, gaining his greatest victory against Saladin at the Battle of Arsuf in September 1197. Saladin made a stand on good territory, with marsh and raised woodland protecting two of his flanks. He then attempted to draw the enemy onto unfavorable ground. Richard wisely held his formation until the right moment, and charged Saladin's weakest flank, winning the day. This turned out to be the high point of Richard's exploits. Saladin's forces were not considerably weakened and were able to regroup to prevent any likelihood of losing Jerusalem to the invaders.

"Richard spent just six months of his reign in England, in which he is reported to have complained about the weather, and spent most of his time raising money from taxes..."

HEROIC FAILURE

Despite Richard's apparent victories and the perception at home, the Third Crusade was a failure. Richard was forced to make peace with Saladin in a treaty that gave his enemy the upper hand. While returning from the Holy Land, he was taken prisoner by the Duke of Austria, who handed him over to one of Richard's greatest adversaries, the Holy Roman Emperor Henry IV, in March 1193. He was imprisoned until a very large ransom of 150,000 marks was raised through taxation. In his absence, his brother John Lackland had ruled in his place. Plotting with Philip II, Richard's former ally, John managed to annoy nobles and commoners alike during his short tenure, which helped foster the idea of Richard as a national hero. However, no sooner had he been freed in 1194 than he was off again, spending his remaining years fighting Philip in France, where he was killed in 1199.

FONDLY REMEMBERED

After his death, Richard became one of the best-loved kings of England, not least because the despised John had returned to the throne. He was a fearless warrior, but his gains were few, and he had little love for England itself. The English needed a hero, having been conquered by the Normans just over a hundred years before; ironically, Richard was barely more English than William the Conqueror.

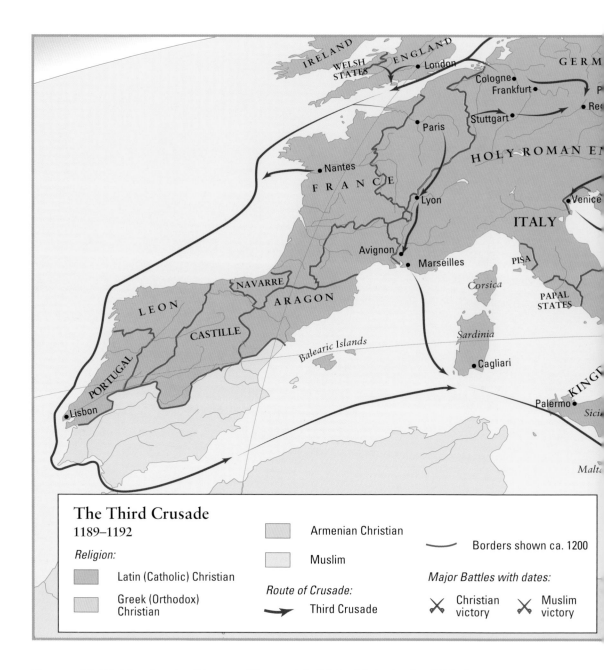

The Third Crusade
1189–1192

Religion:

Latin (Catholic) Christian

Greek (Orthodox) Christian

Armenian Christian

Muslim

Route of Crusade:

Third Crusade

Borders shown ca. 1200

Major Battles with dates:

Christian victory

Muslim victory

The routes of the Third Crusade on the religious map of Europe and the Holy Land during the reign of Richard.

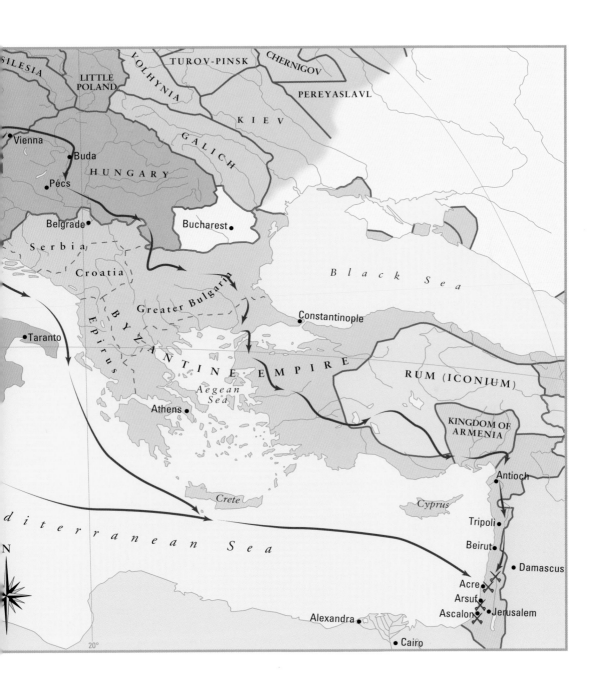

SILESIA

LITTLE
POLAND

VOLHYNIA

TUROV-PINSK

CHERNIGOV

PEREYASLAVL

KIEV

GALICH

Vienna

Buda

HUNGARY

Pécs

Belgrade

Bucharest

Serbia

Croatia

Greater Bulgaria

Black Sea

Taranto

Epirus

BYZANTINE EMPIRE

Constantinople

RUM (ICONIUM)

Aegean
Sea

Athens

KINGDOM OF
ARMENIA

Crete

Cyprus

Antioch

Mediterranean Sea

Tripoli

Beirut

Damascus

Acre

Arsuf

Alexandra

Ascalon

Jerusalem

Cairo

N

20°

Genghis Khan

GENGHIS KHAN, THE GREAT MONGOL EMPEROR, CREATED THE LARGEST CONTINUOUS LAND EMPIRE KNOWN TO HISTORY, AND THE LARGEST EVER EMPIRE TO BE CONTROLLED BY A SINGLE INDIVIDUAL.

Born ca. 1162 and named Temujin, by the time of his death in 1227, Genghis Khan had conquered the vast expanse of Asia westward from the Yellow Sea in China to the Caspian Sea, and from Siberia south to Afghanistan. It was an astonishing feat, conducted by a man whose extraordinary military skills were matched by his political acumen. His ability to control a huge empire while building up its internal political structure meant that the Mongol Empire extended still farther after his death, spreading to Hungary in central Europe.

The early years of Temujin (Genghis' birth name) are subject to some improbable legends, but he certainly did not have the most auspicious childhood, despite being the son of the chieftain of the Borjigin Mongol tribe. The nomadic life of the Mongols was hard, especially for children. At the age of nine, he was sent away from his own family to that of his betrothed, Börte. However, on the death of his father, the boy returned to his tribe to claim the title of chieftain, but his family were expelled and forced to lead a life of extreme poverty within the harsh terrain. At one point, he was captured by the rival Tayichi'ud clan but escaped, which helped establish his reputation. At 16, he finally married Börte, and began his attempts to unify the Mongols and neighboring tribes under his control. Of all his achievements, this proved to be the hardest. Mongolia was a network of khanates and warring tribes in continual conflict with each other; furthermore it was lawless with no central administration. Political affiliations shifted constantly due to arranged marriages, kidnapping, and murders.

ALLIANCES MADE AND UNMADE

The kidnap of Börte by the Merkit tribe saw Temujin seek the assistance of Toghrul, the khan of Kerait, and Jamuha, a childhood friend who had become the khan of the Jadaran. Using Toghrul's forces, Temujin and Jamuha completely defeated the Merkits and freed Börte. Temujin then set about subjugating the Mongols' neighboring foes, including the Naimans, Tatars, and the Jin dynasty that had spread from China in the east. As he made headway, he used various techniques (markedly innovative for the era) to make sure of their loyalty—he delegated powers to the conquered, incorporated their armies into his own and offered them a share of the spoils of war, and made sure that the people were protected from other foes.

Meanwhile, Toghrul and Jamuha began to see the young Temujin as a threat and united against him. Temujin defeated both khans, and by 1206, had managed to unite the Mongols, Keraits, Naimans, Tatars, Merkits, and other local tribes under his rule. He then took the title of "Chingis" more commonly, "Genghis," which means "perfect warrior."

COLOSSAL SLAUGHTER

He now felt strong enough to take on the might of the Jin dynasty, the northern Chinese faction that had effectively ruled the Mongols for hundreds of years. First, he defeated the nearby Tanguts of the Xia dynasty in 1209, opening up the possibility of attacking the Jin on several fronts. With the aid of a Jin traitor, who revealed the position of the enemy, Genghis Khan slaughtered them in their hundreds of thousands at Badger's Mouth in 1211. It is believed that as many as 400,000

Jin soldiers died in one of the bloodiest battles in history. By 1215, Genghis had sacked the Jin capital of Yanying (now Beijing).

So much for the East. Genghis' exploits in the West were no less formidable. His general, Jebe, took the Kara-Khitan Khanate in 1218, while Genghis himself led his forces against the large Khwarezmian Empire of central Asia, which stretched westward to the Caspian Sea and south to the Persian Sea. Its shah had treated Genghis' envoys with disrespect, and his people paid the price in a brutal conquest that involved the slaying of millions. Further victories followed, but with its conclusion in 1220, this was the last monumental conquest by Genghis Khan. He died in 1227 after subjugating the Tangut people to another ferocious onslaught. It is claimed that his murderer was a Tangut princess who castrated him.

Genghis may have promoted those who proved to be loyal, whatever their race or creed, but he was utterly ruthless against those who resisted him, often slaying every single living thing—people and animals alike—in a town that stood in his way. In all, it is believed the Mongol expansion came at the cost of 40 million lives. As a result, he was regarded as a barbarian by his enemies, but his armies were extremely well-disciplined.

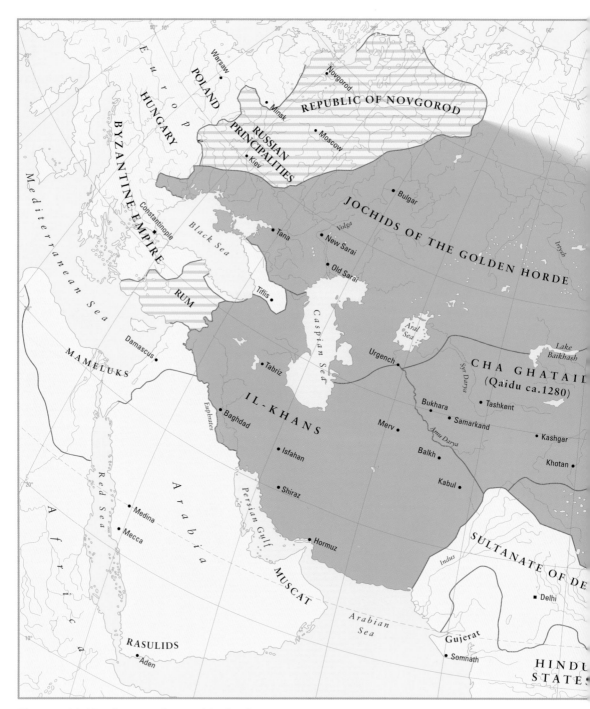

The extent of the Mongol empire in the reign of Genghis Khan.

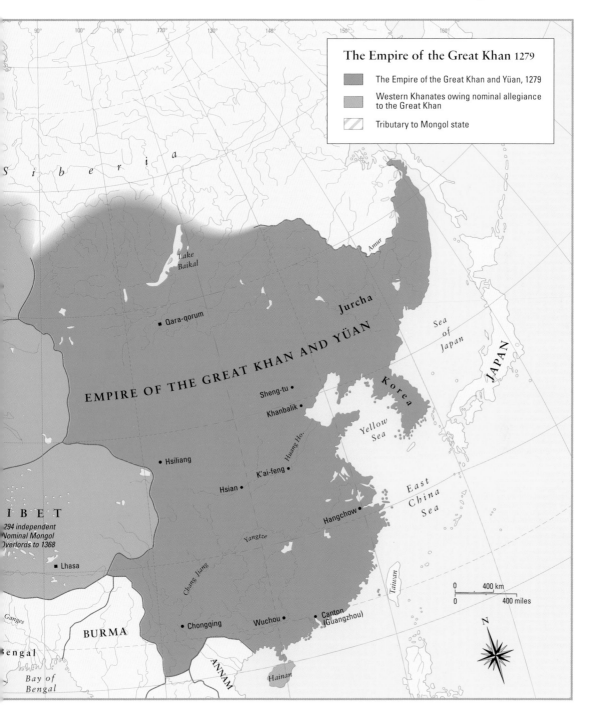

The Empire of the Great Khan 1279

The Empire of the Great Khan and Yüan, 1279

Western Khanates owing nominal allegiance to the Great Khan

Tributary to Mongol state

Siberia

Amur

Lake Baikal

Jurcha

Qara-qorum

Sea of Japan

JAPAN

EMPIRE OF THE GREAT KHAN AND YÜAN

Sheng-tu

Khanbalik

Korea

Yellow Sea

Hsiliang

Huang Ho

Hsian

K'ai-feng

East China Sea

Hangchow

TIBET
294 independent
Nominal Mongol
Overlords to 1368

Yangtze

Lhasa

Chang Jiang

Taiwan

Ganges

Chongqing

Wuchou

Canton
(Guangzhou)

BURMA

0   400 km
0   400 miles

Bengal

ANNAM

N

Bay of
Bengal

Hainan

Robert the Bruce

ROBERT THE BRUCE AND WILLIAM WALLACE FOUGHT IN THE SCOTTISH WARS OF INDEPENDENCE. IT IS THE EXPLOITS OF ROBERT THE BRUCE, HOWEVER, THAT ARE REMEMBERED IN THE UNOFFICIAL NATIONAL ANTHEM OF SCOTLAND.

Robert the Bruce was born on July 11, 1274, the aristocratic grandson of Robert de Brus who was a strong claimant to the Scottish throne. Edward I, the king of England, was asked to arbitrate in the matter of the succession in 1292, and he chose John Balliol over de Brus. However, Edward soon claimed overlordship of all Scotland for himself and demanded that it should supply troops for his war with France. In response, Scotland allied itself to France and attacked the English at Carlisle. Retaliating, Edward I invaded Scotland in 1296, crushing the Scottish forces at the Battle of Dunbar and imprisoning John Balliol in the Tower of London.

At this point, Robert the Bruce appeared to be loyal to Edward—after all, his family believed Balliol to be nothing more than a usurper—but he showed his true colors the following year when he joined the reinvigorated Scottish rebellion. In 1297, William Wallace, a Scottish landowner, assassinated the English High Sheriff of Lanark and then defeated a large English force at the Battle of Stirling Bridge in 1297. Wallace appointed himself as the Guardian of Scotland on behalf of Balliol. However, he risked everything at the Battle of Falkirk in the following year and was defeated. Consequently, he resigned the guardianship in favor of Robert the Bruce and John Comyn, a relative of Balliol and another claimant to the crown.

SEEKING HELP FROM FRANCE

Wallace went to Europe for several years to gain political and financial support for the Scottish cause. Meanwhile, Edward continued his incursions into Scottish territory, and in 1304 finally gained the upper hand. He made John Comyn the sole Guardian as his vassal. Scotland, including Robert the Bruce, had

The strategy at the battle of Bannockburn.

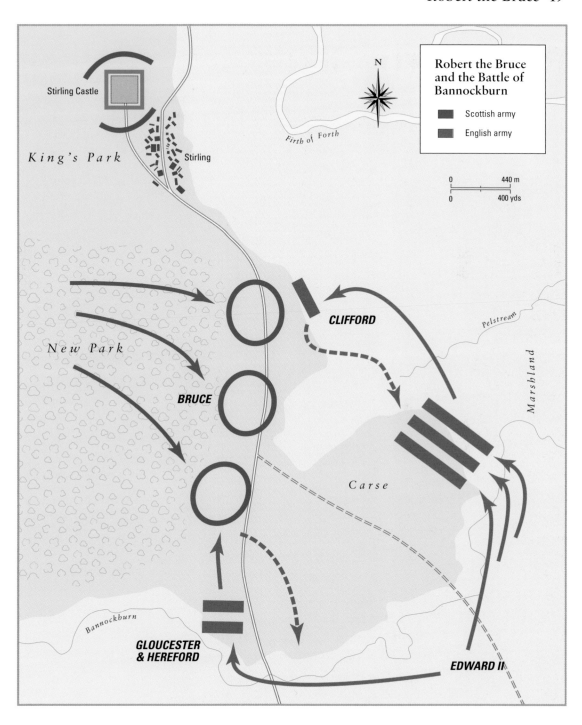

Stirling Castle

King's Park

Stirling

Firth of Forth

N

Robert the Bruce
and the Battle of
Bannockburn

Scottish army

English army

0   440 m
0   400 yds

New Park

CLIFFORD

Pelstream

BRUCE

Marshland

Carse

Bannockburn

GLOUCESTER
& HEREFORD

EDWARD II

A statue of Robert the Bruce at Stirling Castle.

outlawing by Edward I. Robert was unbowed, and was subsequently crowned king of Scotland at Scone in the same year. He was deposed by the English in 1307 and forced to flee to Ireland, but he soon returned with a new strategy to conduct a guerrilla war campaign against the English army, now led by Edward II of England. This led to the pivotal battle of Scottish independence at Bannockburn on June 23–24, 1314.

SEEKING BOGGY GROUND

Robert the Bruce gathered a force of about 7,000 men and positioned them on favorable ground near Stirling Castle, an English stronghold. Most of them were foot soldiers carrying spears, with very little cavalry. The heavily armed English force was much larger, with 16,000 infantry and more than 2,000 cavalry. Robert evened up the odds by making the solid road to Stirling impassable and forcing the English on to the Carse—boggy land near the Bannockburn river.

As the leading section of the English approached, one of their knights, Henry de Bohun, initiated the battle, when he caught sight of Robert armed with only an ax and charged at him on his huge warhorse. Robert stood his ground and felled the knight with a single blow that split his head in two. The Scots then

surrendered, but William Wallace had not. By 1304, he was back in Scotland and continued to be a thorn in Edward's side until his capture in 1305. He was taken to London and hanged, drawn, and quartered in an horrific execution, and his head was placed on a spike on London Bridge.

Wallace was a martyr; Robert was no saint. In 1306, he killed his rival John Comyn during an altercation in a church in Dumfries, leading to his excommunication by the pope and his charged into the English advance, forcing them to retreat, but Bruce wisely stopped his men from following the enemy. On the next day, Edward II and the remaining English army approached through the marshy land. The huge size of the army and the terrain made it difficult for the English to maneuver and they were sitting ducks for the Scottish spearmen—as a result, more than 10,000 English infantrymen were killed, while the Scots suffered only minor losses.

ENGLISH DEFEATED

Edward II had been routed. As the national anthem states, the Scots "sent him homeward to think again." And he did just that. He was wary of ever facing the Scottish in battle again, but he continued to believe that he was their rightful overlord until he was forced to abdicate by the English themselves in 1327. One of the very first acts of his son Edward III was to make peace with Scotland and renounce all claim to Scotland. His place in history guaranteed, Robert the Bruce died on June 7, 1329. Scottish independence from England lasted several hundred years until the 1707 Act of Union.

FACT FILE

Robert the Bruce

Born: July 11, 1274

Died: June 7, 1329

Birthplace: Turnberry, Scotland

Nationality: Scottish

Religion: Roman Catholic

Historic Role: Reputed warrior and king of Scots

Reign: March 1306–June 1329

Marital Alliances: Isabella of Mar, Elizabeth de Burgh

Historic Feats: A great hero of Scottish independence

Legacy: Thanks to Robert the Bruce, King Edward II was wary of ever facing the Scottish in battle again. Scottish independence endured until the Act of Union in 1707

Hero or Villain: Scottish hero

Owain Glyndŵr

THE FOURTEENTH-CENTURY WELSH NATIONALIST OWAIN GLYNDŴR WAS THE FINAL TRUE WELSHMAN TO BE CALLED THE PRINCE OF WALES, A TITLE LATER APPROPRIATED BY THE ENGLISH MONARCHY.

Owain Glyndŵr instigated the Welsh revolt against English rule and holds legendary status for many Welsh nationalists. After his campaign for full Welsh independence faltered, he disappeared and his final years are shrouded in mystery. Born in the 1350s into the Welsh aristocracy, he was sent to London to study and practice law before returning to Wales in 1383. His anti-Englishness was not yet evident and he undertook three years of military service in England in 1384, fighting against the Scottish and gaining invaluable experience for his later campaigns. It is likely that he assisted his latter-day adversary Henry Bolingbroke against Richard II at the Battle of Radcot Bridge before returning to Wales to lead an ostensibly quiet life.

Owain was not a natural rebel looking for a fight—he was provoked. He had a fractious relationship with his English neighbor, the scheming Baron Grey de Ruthyn. He was an ally of Henry Bolingbroke, who had secured the throne of England and become Henry IV. Matters came to a head in 1400, when Grey seized some of Owain's land, and then he failed to inform Owain of a royal order to supply Henry IV with troops for the ongoing conflict on the Scottish border. As a result, Owain was deemed a traitor.

The Welsh rebellion and the routes taken by all sides in conflict.

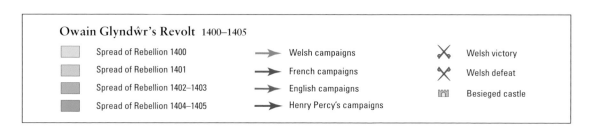

Owain Glyndŵr's Revolt 1400–1405

Spread of Rebellion 1400	→ Welsh campaigns	✗ Welsh victory
Spread of Rebellion 1401	→ French campaigns	✗ Welsh defeat
Spread of Rebellion 1402–1403	→ English campaigns	🏰 Besieged castle
Spread of Rebellion 1404–1405	→ Henry Percy's campaigns	

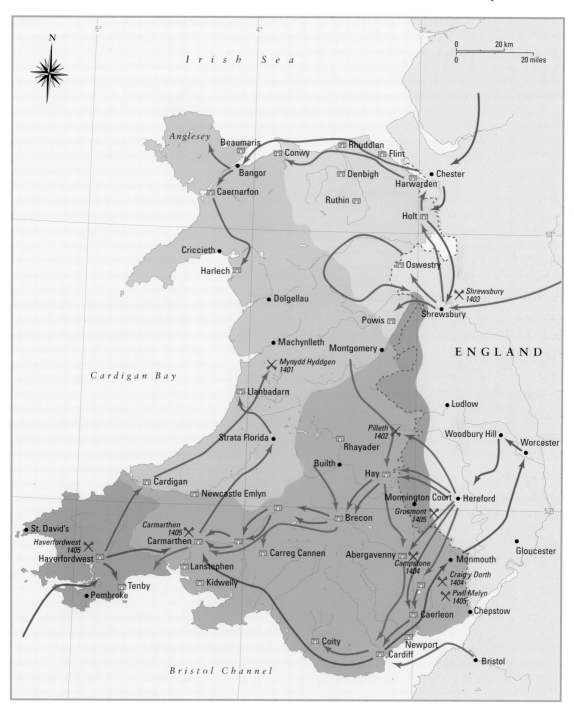

In retaliation, Owain's supporters proclaimed him Prince of Wales on September 16, 1400, and he duly attacked Grey's castle. Henry IV moved against Owain to quell the rebellion, but disgruntled Welsh nationalists, particularly in the center and north of Wales, joined his cause and the Welsh Revolt began to gain momentum. Owain scored an impressive victory at Mynydd Hyddgen in 1401, and gained further support after the English parliament unwisely passed the Penal Laws, under which Welshmen were forbidden to bear arms, take senior public office or buy property in England.

> *Disgruntled Welsh nationalists ...joined his cause and the Welsh Revolt began to gain momentum. Owain scored an impressive victory at Mynydd Hyddgen in 1401...*

ALLIED TO MORTIMER

In 1402, Owain achieved what was probably his most enjoyable feat—the capture of Baron Grey de Ruthyn. He held him prisoner for a year before forcing Henry IV to pay a ransom. He also captured Sir Edmund Mortimer, but Henry refused to pay his ransom because Mortimer was a rival to his own throne. In fact, Owain realized that he had found an ally in Mortimer and allowed him to marry his daughter. Over the course of the following year, the Welsh Revolt reached its zenith and became a truly national affair. Welshmen in England, including soldiers, left their positions to join Owain's forces. By 1404, he was held in such esteem throughout Wales that he was able to hold court at Harlech Castle, appoint a chancellor, and call his first Welsh parliament, during which he was officially ordained as the Prince of Wales. He was already starting to plan the structure of an independent Wales, laying down provision for a Welsh Church and university system. Owain set about trying to secure the future of his country by striking an alliance with Mortimer and Henry Percy, the rebellious Earl of Northumberland. They agreed the Tripartite Indenture, in which Owain would control Wales while the two Englishmen would divide England. Of course, this would all depend on the removal of Henry IV. To this end, the Welsh became allied to the French, who were also at war with Henry.

MYSTERIOUS ENALLIED WITH THE FRENCH

Owain allowed the French to land at Milford Haven in Wales in order to march into England toward Worcester, but the English avoided battle and the French soon withdrew. Their own political climate was shifting toward peace with England—at just the wrong time for Owain. Perhaps the lack of French action took the heart out of the Welsh rebellion. In 1406, they suffered a series of defeats, and the English took the Isle of Anglesey in north Wales. Henry IV's son, Henry of Monmouth, also changed his father's preferred strategy for all-out battle. He used the remaining English castles in Wales to impose economic blockades on various parts of the region. It became a war of attrition, which was concentrated on denying arms and supplies to the rebels, before using his forces to secure an area.

MYSTERIOUS END

While Owain was marshalling his forces to seek bigger confrontations with the English, the Welsh lords at home were beginning to surrender. Even Harlech fell to the English in 1409. Mortimer was killed, and Owain's wife and daughters were taken off and imprisoned in the Tower of London.

Owain led a series of successful minor ambushes against the English in 1412, but after that point he was never seen again, nor was he ever betrayed. To this day his burial place remains unknown. By then, the Welsh Revolt was over. His disappearance became the stuff of legend, and Wales returned to its uneasy but stable relationship with England.

FACT FILE

Owain Glyndŵr

Born: ca. 1349 or 1359

Died: ca. 1416

Nationality: Welsh

Parents: Gruffudd Fychan II (ca. 1330–1369) and Elen ferch Tomas ap Llywelyn (ca. 1337–13??)

Historic Role: Welsh nationalist and instigator of the Welsh Revolt

Reign: 1401–ca. 1416

Marital Alliances: Margaret Hanmer (or Marred ferch Dafydd), Princess of Wales (1383)

Historic Feats: Glyndŵr captured Baron Grey de Ruthyn in 1402, forcing Henry IV to pay a ransom. He held court at Harlech Castle after 1404 and gained mass support for the Welsh Revolt

Circumstances of Death: Glyndŵr disappeared after 1412. The circumstances of his death are unknown

Hero or Villain: A hero of the Welsh Revolt

Joan of Arc

AT A TIME WHEN WOMEN WERE NOT
ALLOWED TO HOLD ANY OFFICE OF
AUTHORITY, 17-YEAR-OLD JOAN OF ARC
LED THE FRENCH ARMY INTO BATTLE
AND WON.

Members of the French Church
believed that Joan, this
apparently divinely inspired
young woman was a heretical witch and
burnt her to death before she reached her
twentiy-first birthday. Whether saintly,
satanic, or schizophrenic, she changed the
course of the Hundred Years' War.

Jeanne d'Arc (or Joan of Arc as she is
known in the English-speaking world)
was born around 1412 in Domrémy in
Lorraine, northeast France. The daughter
of a farmer, her education would have
amounted to little more than spinning
wool and tending her father's flocks, but
she was heading for a more adventurous
life. She was filled with religious fervor,
and believed that she had been given a
mission from God to defeat the English

The stategic positions at the siege of Orléans.

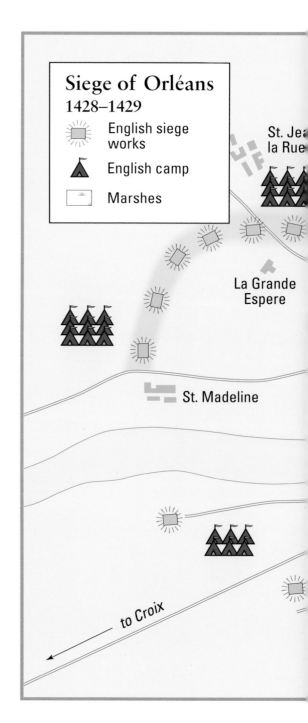

Siege of Orléans
1428–1429

English siege works

English camp

Marshes

St. Je...
la Rue...

La Grande
Espere

St. Madeline

to Croix

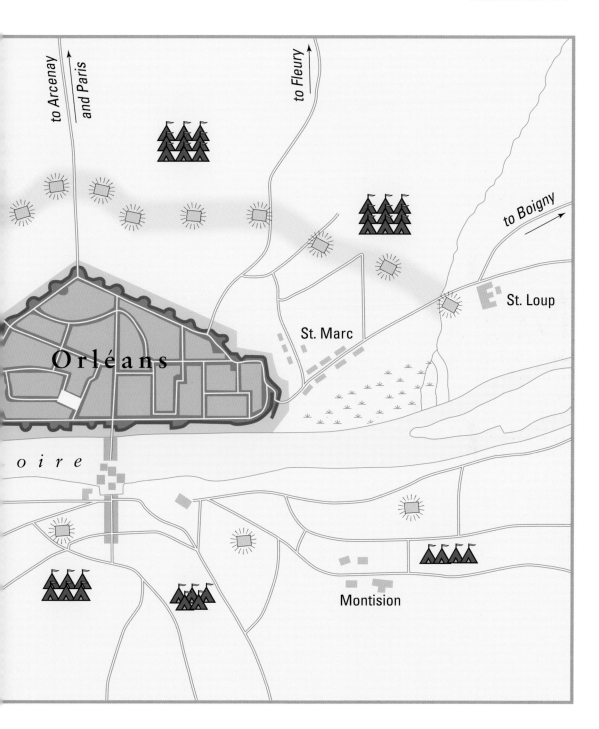

to Arcenay and Paris

to Fleury

to Boigny

St. Loup

St. Marc

Orléans

oire

Montision

A memorial to Joan of Arc, the Maid of Orléans.

managed to occupy much of northern France. He also formed an important alliance with the Burgundians. After the deaths of both Charles VI and Henry V in 1422, the infant son of Henry V was left the nominal king of both England and France (Henry VI). By 1429, the Dauphin Charles, the French heir, seemed almost powerless to defeat the alliance, especially because the English had taken Paris and were now besieging the all-important city of Orléans. Many feared that if Orléans fell, so would all of France.

DIVINE INSPIRATION

Hearing voices in her head, Joan believed that she had receiving instructions directly from angels since she was 13. She was granted an audience with the Dauphin in Chinon and, somewhat incredibly, Charles was persuaded to hand over the control of some of his forces to this illiterate self-proclaimed virgin warrior. He was a desperate man. Joan proceeded to join a relief force that was raised to aid the besieged city of Orléans. This unlikeliest of military leaders, who shaved off her hair and donned a suit of armor, managed to rally the exhausted troops with her visionary fervor. She turned the Anglo-French war into a religious conflict, leading the troops into battle under the banner "Party of the Kingdom of Heaven."

army that occupied northern France, and to make sure that Charles, the Dauphin, was crowned king of France. France had been in the grip of the Hundred Years War for more than 90 years by this point. It had begun as a dispute over the succession to the throne, with both the English and the Burgundians claiming the right to rule France. English King Henry V gained a huge victory over the French monarch Charles VI at Agincourt in 1415 and

Succeeding where experienced generals had failed, she relieved the city of Orléans in May 1229 and then defeated the English at Patay, to the north of the city. The English success at Agincourt had been led by their skillful, accurate archers, but she attacked before the English had time to get them into position. She decimated the main body of the army, slaughtered the archers, and killed many of the English commanders while suffering minimal losses. The English lost around 2,500 men, while only 100 Frenchmen were killed or wounded. The victory allowed the Dauphin to be crowned Charles VII in Reims in July just as Joan had predicted. From then on, Joan was known as the Maid of Orléans.

So far so good, in this tale of an unlikely military genius, but the angels had also given her warning that she would suffer a series of defeats. Her success began to falter when she failed to capture Paris in September and was wounded in the leg by a crossbow. Then, while helping to relieve the besieged town of Compiègne in May 1430, she was captured by the Burgundians. They sold her to their English allies, who were still hurting from the defeat she had inflicted at Patay

and believed that the voices in her head came from Satan rather than God. They imprisoned Joan for a year.

MARTYRDOM AND CANONIZATION
Her bitter end came when a tribunal of churchmen led by Bishop Pierre Cauchon of Beauvais, who supported the English, found her guilty of heresy and witchcraft. She was burnt to death while tied to a pillar in Rouen on 30 May 1431. The English may have succeeded in having Joan killed, but her victories against them had greatly weakened their position at a pivotal moment. The Burgundians soon switched sides and the English were forced to slowly withdraw from France.

The French churchmen, who could not believe that this young woman had a closer relationship with God than they themselves, may not have accepted Joan's claims to divinity, but over the centuries she continued to gain support in the Catholic Church. In 1456, Pope Callixtus III declared that she was innocent of heresy and was, therefore, a martyr. She was canonized in 1920, becoming St. Joan of Arc. She remains a national heroine and patron saint of France.

> *Her end came when a tribunal of churchmen led by Bishop Cauchon who supported the English, found her guilty of heresy and witchcraft. She was burnt to death ...*

Tomás de Torquemada

NOT MANY MONKS ARE VIEWED AS
VILLAINS, BUT THE LEADER OF THE
SPANISH INQUISITION, WHO HAD
AT LEAST **2,000** PEOPLE KILLED AS
SUPPOSED HERETICS, HAS TO BE ONE.

Torquemada, born in Valladolid, Spain in 1420, became a Dominican monk before being appointed prior of the monastery of Santa Cruz in Segovia. It was there that he began his life-changing relationship with the young Infanta Isabella, the heir to the kingdom of Castile. Torquemada became her confessor and soon had her complete confidence. In a wise political move, he advised her to marry King Ferdinand of Aragón in 1469, thereby uniting Spain under their joint rule. When she acceded to the throne of Castile in 1474, he was one of her most trusted advisors.

The Catholics in Spain at that time felt that they were under threat from

The medieval political and religious map of Spain and Portugal.

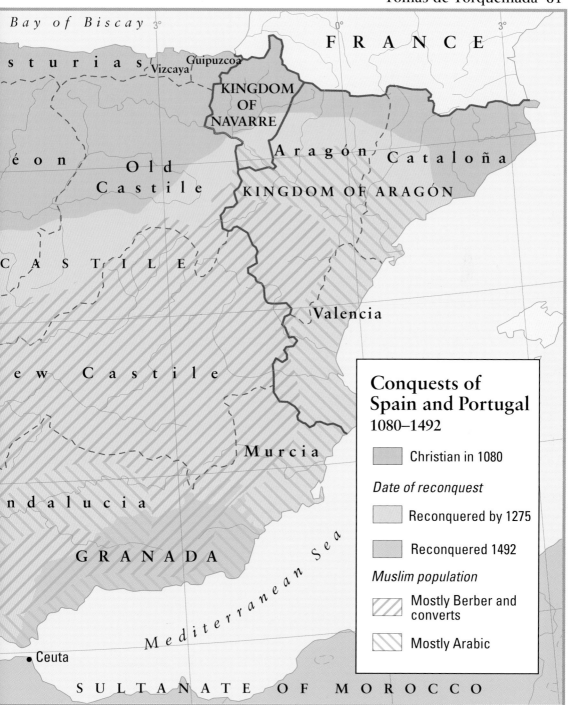

Bay of Biscay

FRANCE

sturias

Vizcaya Guipuzcoa

KINGDOM
OF
NAVARRE

Aragón Cataloña

éon

Old
Castile

KINGDOM OF ARAGÓN

CASTILE

Valencia

ew Castile

Murcia

ndalucia

GRANADA

Mediterranean Sea

Ceuta

SULTANATE OF MOROCCO

Conquests of
Spain and Portugal
1080–1492

Christian in 1080

Date of reconquest

Reconquered by 1275

Reconquered 1492

Muslim population

Mostly Berber and
converts

Mostly Arabic

the Jewish Marranos, who had gained increasing financial, political, and religious influence, and the Muslim Mariscos. To have full legal entitlements, both Muslims and Jews had been forced to convert to Catholicism. Torquemada suspected the Marranos of plotting to convert the whole of Spain to the Jewish faith, and convinced both Isabella and Pope Sixtus IV to set up an Inquisition in 1478. The Church believed that the Jews, in particular, had undertaken sham conversions, and decided to test the resolve of the Catholic converts. This first wave of the Inquisition was responsible for great cruelty while achieving little, partly because there was no central administrative overseer.

One early nineteenth-century religious historian, Bishop Juan Antonio Loorente, estimated that 8,800 people were killed by fire during Torquemada's Inquisition.

THE GRAND INQUISITOR

In 1483, Isabella instructed Torquemada to revive the Inquisition into the faith of converts. With the blessing of Pope Sixtus IV, Torquemada himself took the title of the Grand Inquisitor and set up a range of tribunals in the kingdoms of Castile and Aragón, including in the cities of Seville, Valladolid, Jaén, Ciudad Real, Avila, Cordova, and Zaragoza. All appeals against the verdicts of the tribunals had to go directly to him, and he was assisted by a High Council. Torquemada, a fanatical bigot, approached the new phase of the Inquisition with zeal, never questioning the religiosity of his actions.

He set out 28 articles to guide his inquisitors as they sought out any trace of the converts' heresy, renunciation of Catholicism, sodomy, sorcery, and usury (the practice of lending money at unreasonably high rates, a claim often made against Jews). He also permitted the use of torture to extract confessions. He incited the Catholic populace to work as spies on their "non-believing" neighbors, and would torture any Jew accused of heresy by two other citizens. If they did not confess to still practicing their original faith, they were executed; there was little or no prospect of being found innocent, no matter how weak the evidence or how biased the claim. Many were burnt at the stake, others were beheaded, while some died in prison. In a bizarre theatrical touch, the condemned were forced to wear a cloak adorned with the flames of hell.

One early nineteenth-century religious historian, Bishop Juan Antonio Llorente, estimated that 8,800 people were killed by fire during Torquemada's Inquisition, and another 9,000 were subjected to other cruel punishments. These figures are probably an exaggeration, and the total number of deaths is thought to be closer to 2,000.

These executions were not enough for Torquemada, who wanted every single member of the Jewish faith to be removed from Spain. His Inquisition only had jurisdiction over Jewish and Muslim converts over the age of 12. Those who had not converted may not have enjoyed the full rights of citizenship, but they were untouchable and this pained Torquemada. His influence over both Isabella and Ferdinand remained strong, so he was able to convince them to declare an edict in March 1492 demanding the expulsion of all the remaining Jews in Spain. A total of some 40,000 Jews soon left the Iberian Peninsula, taking with them their trading skills and prosperity.

"THE HAMMER OF HERETICS"
The Inquisition was originally popular with Spanish Catholics, with contemporary chronicler Sebastian de Olmedo calling Torquemada "the hammer of heretics, the light of Spain, the saviour of his country." However, critics began to emerge once it was realized that his zealousness meant that the converts were being killed without a fair hearing. Before long, Torquemada had to travel with an armed guard of several hundred men in case he was ambushed. The new

pope, Alexander IV, even appointed assistant inquisitors to try to temper Torquemada's sanctimonious cruelty. In fact, his decimation of the Jewish population through fire and exile was not only bigoted and cruel, but led to great financial disadvantage for Spain, whose economy relied on their skills and financial acumen.

Torquemada died on September 16, 1498, no doubt believing that he had done God's work.

FACT FILE

Tomás de Torquemada

Born: 1420

Died: September 16, 1498

Birthplace: Valladolid, Spain

Religion: Catholic

Historic Role: Spanish monk, confessor to Queen Isabella, and leader of the Spanish Inquisition

Objective: To eliminate Judaism and Islam in Spain via forced conversion and expulsion

Legacy: Torquemada was responsible for torture and thousands of deaths; the expulsion of the Jewish population led to great financial disadvantage for Spain

Hero or Villain: Villain

Vlad the Impaler

VLAD III OF WALLACHIA WAS KNOWN BY TWO NAMES THAT HINT AT HIS CRUELTY AND THE FEAR HE INSPIRED. THE FIRST NAME IS VLAD THE IMPALER, FROM HIS FAVORED METHOD OF DESPATCHING HIS VICTIMS; THE SECOND IS DRACULA.

In fact, Dracula was a family name. His father was Vlad Dracul (meaning "Vlad the Dragon" in Romanian), so he became known as Vlad Dracula—Vlad, son of the Dragon. The elder Vlad had received the title when he was inducted into the Order of the Dragon. Rather than some sort of satanic organization, this was a chivalric order of Christian knights who swore to defend the cross from the Ottoman Turks. Vlad Dracula himself would join the order and fight the Ottomans, but it was his sadism that led to the word "Dracula" becoming synonymous with pure malevolence, especially after Bram Stoker used Vlad as the inspiration for his vampiric novel of 1897. The fictional Dracula was something of a part-timer compared with the real one, whose victims numbered 80,000.

Vlad was born in Transylvania (in modern-day Romania) in 1431. His father, Vlad II, was the leader of neighboring Wallachia. The Ottoman Turks were the power in the region, with their burgeoning empire stretching to the Balkans. In order to keep his throne, Vlad II had to pay taxes to the Ottoman sultan and send two of his younger sons, Vlad and Radu, to the Ottoman court as hostages. Vlad spent three years there and was often whipped and beaten for his defiance, which may go some way to explaining his own cruelty and cynicism as an adult. Wallachia was also under constant threat from Hungarian ruler John Hunyadi, who killed Vlad II in 1447 and blinded Vlad's elder brother before burying him alive. In response, the Ottomans invaded Wallachia and put the 16-year-old Vlad on the throne. However, the first rule of Vlad III was short-lived, as John Hunyadi gained the upper hand and made his ally, Vladislav, the pupper ruler.

EXCESSIVE CRUELTY

Vlad fled to Moldavia, but in 1456 returned to conquer Wallachia, killing Vladislav with his own hands in close

Wallachia and the regions surrounding it during the time of Vlad the Impaler.

combat. As ruler, Vlad's skills—and his cruelty—soon came to the fore. Putting in place strong administrative measures to rebuild a territory ruined by years of conflict, he also introduced new laws to administer excessive punishment on criminals. Vlad systematically removed the troublesome nobility whose shifting allegiances had long caused difficulties in Wallachia. He killed dozens of them, while creating his own personal bodyguard made up of terrifying mercenaries. They began raids into Transylvania to kill other rival noblemen and also wiped out Saxon settlers, using Vlad's favorite technique of executing them by impaling on stakes.

Vlad knew that the local slaughtering would never be enough to secure the kingdom, because the main threat continued to be the Ottoman Empire.

FACT FILE

Vlad the Impaler

Born: 1431

Died: 1476

Birthplace: Sighisoara, Transylvania

Historical Role: Prince of Wallachia

Reigns: 1448; 1456–1462; 1476

Historic Exploits: Conquered Wallachia in 1456; removed rival noblemen and Saxon settlers by impaling them on stakes; advanced across the Danube and through modern-day Bulgaria in 1462, wiping out the sultan's army. His victims numbered 80,000

Circumstances of Death: Assassinated by the Ottomans in 1476

Hero or Villain: Villain

In 1459, when Sultan Mehmet II sent envoys to collect the regular tax on Wallachia, Vlad refused to pay. Not only that, because the envoys had not removed their turbans in his presence, he had them nailed to their heads. This was a man who enjoyed his innovations as he took the lives of others. Mehmet sent an army, including 10,000 cavalry, into Wallachia to subdue Dracula, but he surrounded them as they rode through a narrow pass and captured almost the entire force. Showing no mercy, he had them all impaled. With sardonic deference to rank, he saved the tallest stake for the army's general, the aristocratic Hamza Pasha.

RAVAGING THE LAND

Vlad now had a fearsome reputation both at home and abroad. In 1462, he swept across the Danube and through modern-day Bulgaria, ravaging the Ottoman-held land. He admitted in a letter to Matthias Corvinus, the new king of Hungary, that he had "killed peasants, men and women, young and old ... killed 23,884 Turks without counting those we burned in homes or those whose heads were cut off by our soldiers." He wanted to provoke the sultan into an all-out war, and Mehmet duly complied. He sent a force of 90,000 against Vlad's army of half that size, but was soundly beaten, losing 15,000 men in

Vlad's castle, where the legend of Count Dracula has its origins.

a single battle. At one point, the sultan is said to have found the bodies of 20,000 of his countryman impaled on a forest of stakes. He retreated.

In the end, it was Vlad's own brother, Radu—who had remained loyal to the Ottomans since his captivity—who eventually defeated Vlad in 1462. By this time, Vlad was struggling for money and resources, while Radu was well-supplied with both by the wealthy and grateful

> *...he swept across the Danube and through modern-day Bulgaria, ravaging the Ottoman-held land. He admitted in a letter to Matthias Corvinus to killing 23,884 Turks...*

Ottomans. Vlad went to Hungary to seek financial assistance from Matthias Corvinus, but the Hungarian seized him and imprisoned him for at least ten years, taking him out of action. After the death of his brother Radu in 1475, Vlad attempted a reconquest of Wallachia, but he was assassinated by the Ottomans in 1476. His head was carried in triumph to the Ottoman capital of Constantinople.

Lucrezia Borgia

THERE ARE TWO VERSIONS OF THE CHARACTER OF LUCREZIA BORGIA. WAS SHE A RELIGIOUS CHARITABLE GENTLEWOMAN, OR A *FEMME FATALE* DISPENSING POISON FROM A HOLLOWED-OUT RING?

The Borgias were one of the major families in Italian politics in the fifteenth and sixteenth centuries, but the story of their rule is dominated by tales of incest, murder, and the abuse of power. Cesare Borgia was the illegitimate son of Rodrigo Borgia—otherwise known as the supposedly celibate Pope Alexander VI—who was so corrupt that he thought nothing of making Cesare a cardinal when he was only 17. Cesare was a ruthless and treacherous man who left the priesthood to pursue power, fighting the city-republics of Italy. He became the evil model for Machiavelli's *The Prince*, and thought nothing of resorting to poison or the assassin's blade to remove his rivals.

The life of Cesare's sister Lucrezia was supposedly no less scandalous, with many legends that picture her as a murderer and poisoner, as well as an incestuous and promiscuous lover. The tales are historically dubious, but the whole Borgia family was far from saintly and stories of a female villain have long held a particular allure. Born in 1480, she was another illegitimate child of Pope Alexander VI and grew into a fabled beauty, with pale skin, long blonde hair, and hazel eyes. She was a pawn in Alexander's machinations, and he used her for political effect by arranging convenient marriage alliances. At the age of 13, she was married off to Giovanni Sforza, a member of the most powerful family in Milan. This allowed Alexander to create a strong alliance against Alfonso, the king of Naples. However, Pope Alexander was fickle in his political associations and changed sides in 1496, necessitating the annulment of Lucrezia's marriage. Giovanni at first refused to comply, and accused the Borgias of incest, but in the end he was forced to sign a confession of his sexual impotence, which paved the way for an annulment.

Alexander then betrothed Lucrezia to Alonso of Aragon, the young, illegitimate

The political map of Italy during the heyday of the Borgias.

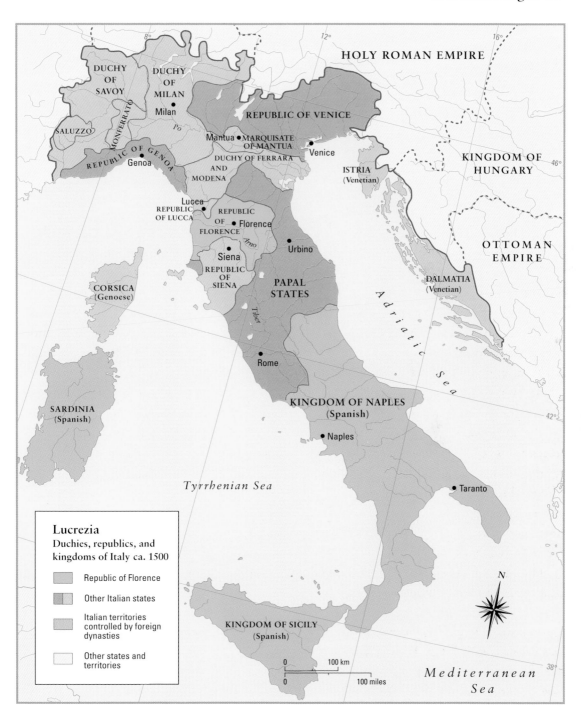

HOLY ROMAN EMPIRE

DUCHY OF SAVOY

DUCHY OF MILAN
Milan

SALUZZO

MONFERRATO

REPUBLIC OF GENOA
Genoa

Po

REPUBLIC OF VENICE

Mantua • MARQUISATE OF MANTUA

DUCHY OF FERRARA AND MODENA

Venice

ISTRIA (Venetian)

KINGDOM OF HUNGARY

46°

REPUBLIC OF LUCCA
Lucca

REPUBLIC OF FLORENCE
Florence

Arno

Urbino

OTTOMAN EMPIRE

Siena

REPUBLIC OF SIENA

PAPAL STATES

Tiber

Adriatic Sea

DALMATIA (Venetian)

CORSICA (Genoese)

Rome

SARDINIA (Spanish)

KINGDOM OF NAPLES (Spanish)

42°

Naples

Tyrrhenian Sea

Taranto

Lucrezia
Duchies, republics, and kingdoms of Italy ca. 1500

Republic of Florence

Other Italian states

Italian territories controlled by foreign dynasties

Other states and territories

N

KINGDOM OF SICILY (Spanish)

0   100 km

0   100 miles

Mediterranean Sea

38°

Portrait of a Woman *by Bartolomeo Veneto, traditionally assumed to be Lucrezia Borgia.*

both Cesare and Alexander acknowledged paternity of the child, but it seems unlikely that Lucrezia was actually the mother.

MARRIED OFF AGAIN

Despite this supposed pregnancy, Lucrezia and Alfonso married in the Vatican in 1498 when she was 18. They fell in love and had a son. However, the Borgias shifted allegiances yet again, this time toward France, the enemy of Naples. Alfonso was all too aware of Cesare's reputation and fled Rome in 1499.

The Borgias forced Lucrezia to lure him back to the city, and in 1500 Cesare's hired men attempted to assassinate Alfonso, stabbing him in the head, arm, and leg. He survived, but the vengeful Cesare had his henchmen strangle Alfonso while he was recovering in bed. Lucrezia was enraged but powerless to seek retribution.

Two years later, she was married off again, this time to Alfonso d'Este. She was only 21 and already on her third marriage. This was the Borgias' greatest nuptial machination, because Alfonso was the heir of the powerful duke of Ferrara.

Finally satisfied, the Borgias ended the ritual of marrying Lucrezia off and then removing her husband, and she was able to sustain her marriage to Alfonso while having five further children. The chance of her being able to pursue a

son of the king of Naples. However, it is claimed that prior to the marriage Lucrezia, who was staying in a convent for her supposed safe-keeping, became pregnant by a handsome, young servant called Perotto. The short-tempered and insanely jealous Cesare promptly killed Perotto, while the disgruntled Sforza family spread the rumor that Cesare was the real father of the child. The rumors did not stop there—it was claimed that Lucrezia also had a sexual relationship with her own father, the pope. In fact, settled family life greatly increased when Pope Alexander died in 1503. Neither Alfonso nor Lucrezia was faithful, with the latter having affairs with the Marquess of Mantua and the poet Pietro Bembo, but their union was solid. In her husband's occasional absences, Lucrezia proved to be a good administrator of Ferrara, while her court became the cultural center of the Renaissance. She was the patron of acclaimed artist Titian, and her court was frequented by many

Her court became a cultural centre... She was a patron of acclaimed artist Titian and her court was frequented by many of the greatest poets and artists of the era.

of the greatest poets and artists of the era. By the time she died of puerperal fever at 39, Lucrezia was known as the "Good Duchess" because she had founded hospitals and schools, and she engaged in charitable work—hardly the epitaph of a conniving murderer. Nevertheless, the unsubstantiated tales of incest became the fodder of legends. In truth, Cesare and Pope Alexander were the real villains of the Borgia family.

FACT FILE

Lucrezia Borgia

Born: April 18, 1480

Died: June 24, 1519

Birthplace: Subiaco, Italy

Historic Period: Italian Renaissance

Parents: Cardinal Rodrigo Borgia, the future Pope Alexander VI (ca. 1431–1503) and Vannozza dei Cattanei (1442–1518)

Marital Alliances: Giovanni Sforza, Lord of Pesaro and Count of Catignola (1493–1496); Alonso of Aragon, Duke of Bisceglie (1498–1500); Alfonso d'Este, Duke of Ferrara (1501–1519)

Historic Feats: Borgia's court was the cultural epicenter of the Renaissance. In later life, she engaged in charitable work and earned the title of "the Good Duchess"

Circumstances of Death: Puerperal fever

Legacy: The myths surrounding Lucrezia's existence form the basis of fictional biographies, movies, and opera

Hero or Villain: Uncertain: *femme fatale* versus political pawn for the Borgia family

EARLY MODERN WORLD

Spanning centuries and colored by the Renaissance, reform, and revolutions, the early modern period was a time of great conquests and great upheaval; its heroes and villains emerged from around the globe. Bloodlust seems to be a key element in an understanding of the likes of Russia's notorious Czar Ivan the Terrible, Transylvanian countess Elizabeth Báthory, and terrifying English pirate Blackbeard. Reform of Russia was at the heart of Czar Peter the Great's accomplishment, while revolution was key to the legends of the first American president George Washington and French revolutionary Robespierre. Heroes or villains? Sometimes even history cannot answer this question.

Ivan the Terrible

RUSSIAN RULER IVAN WAS POSSIBLY DERANGED, WITH A FERVOR THAT VEERED BETWEEN RELIGIOSITY AND WANTON BLOODSHED, BUT HE BECAME THE FIRST CZAR OF ALL RUSSIA AND LAID THE FOUNDATIONS FOR THE RUSSIAN EMPIRE.

Terror and acts of violence, including the murder of his own son, stained his reign to the extent that he became known as Ivan the Terrible. Ivan was born on August 25, 1530 in Kolomenskoye near Moscow, and was crowned Ivan IV, Grand Duke of Moscow, at the age of three. However, he had to wait until the grand old age of 14 before he could assume power in 1544. He felt that his reign was often threatened by the boyars (the local nobles) when he was a child. At the age of 16 he was crowned as the first czar of Russia, uniting the ethnic Russians under the same leadership.

As the first ruler of the huge expanse of Russia, he attempted to centralize power in Moscow. By the age of 19, he had set up the first national assembly. He reformed the legal code, the structure of the Church, and local administration, all within his first decade as czar. He established the first printing press in Russia, for the publication of religious works, and in the mid-1550s began construction of St. Basil's Cathedral, which remains one of the great buildings in Moscow. Yet even this achievement is marred by tales of Ivan's brutality. He was so impressed with the design of the cathedral that he had its architect blinded, so that he could never design another building that would rival it.

MAKING ALLIANCES

As well as overseeing matters of the internal administration of Russia, Ivan was also outward-looking, establishing trade with Elizabeth I of England. His missives to Elizabeth are almost love letters, forming the basis of a relationship between the Russian and English monarchies that would only cease with the execution of the final czar of Russia, Nicholas II, in 1918. However, Ivan's expansive relationships with other nation-states were less chivalric. His ambition was to create an enormous empire. He was not content to rule over just the ethnic Russians, and as a result, he

Expansion of Russia under Ivan the IV and beyond ca. 1530–1613

■ Russia, ca. 1530	*1584* Date of conquest	→ Unsuccessful military foray against Crimean Tatars, 1556–1559	→ Polish and Lithuanian campaign in Livonian War, 1579–1581
■ Russian gains to 1613	• *1584* Date of settlement	→ Yermak's route into Siberia, 1581–1584	→ Ivan IV's campaign
	KIRGIZ People, tribe		

The extent and expansion of the Russian empire from 1530 to 1613.

pushed into the lands of other races, the control of which would become a feature of Russian rule for centuries to come.

First, he campaigned against the Muslim Tatars, conquering Kazan with an army of 150,000 men in 1552. Almost all the residents of Kazan, the Tatar capital, were massacred. Additionally, the Tatar state of Astrakhan was conquered by Ivan four years later, and Russia thereby became

Russian icon-style painting of Ivan the Terrible.

a multinational state of diverse religions and cultures. Ivan's desire for power over as much land as possible drew him westward into the long Livonian War against the Livonians, Lithuanians, Swedes, and Poles, which lasted 24 years, from 1558, without bringing any appreciable gains. In his later years, he also conquered the vast expanse of Siberia with the help of the Cossack leader Yermak Timofeyevich.

DEBAUCHERY AND RELIGIOUS AUSTERITY

Despite his reputation for terror, Ivan was to write to Prince Kurbsky in 1577, toward the end of his life, "Did I ascend to the throne by robbery or armed bloodshed? I was born to rule by the grace of God."

He may have come to power in Moscow by right, but the grace of God did not always seem apparent in his lust for power, which was marked by war, executions, and terror. His entire reign proved to be brutal, but his final years seemed particularly bloody, and are responsible for his epithet of "the Terrible," meaning terrifying rather than bad or incapable.

He managed to combine both debauchery and religious austerity while conducting a campaign of hatred against the boyars. Ivan created his own, nonhereditary ruling class to replace the boyars. Many of the 12,000 boyars were executed on trumped-up charges of conspiracy, and many others were expelled. The new ruling class, known as the *Oprichniki*, subjected the peasants to terrible oppression and high taxes, to the extent that many fled Russia.

MENTALLY UNSTABLE

Ivan took particular exception to the noblemen of the prosperous city of Novgorod, suspecting them of preparing to defect to Lithuania during the futile Livonian War. In 1570, he ordered the *Oprichniki* to sack the city. They virtually destroyed it by fire, killing 1,500 members of the nobility, and at least the same number of innocent peasants. Many survivors of the outrageous pillaging found themselves deported from the city.

By this time, Ivan's mental health appeared to be driving him toward increasingly irrational behavior. He married no less than five times in the 1570s, getting rid of each wife, in turn, through murder or by forcing them into a convent. In 1581, for instance, he beat his pregnant daughter-in-law, causing her to miscarry. When his son Ivan Ivanovich remonstrated with him, Ivan killed him in a fit of rage. The younger Ivan had been regarded as his only viable heir. Instead, when Ivan the Terrible died on March 28, 1584, control of the empire passed to his younger son, Feodor, who was mentally disabled. As a consequence, the empire suffered and what is known as "the Time of Troubles" began.

The new ruling class, known as the Oprichniki, subjected the peasants to terrible oppression and high taxes, to the extent that many fled Russia.

FACT FILE

Ivan the Terrible

Born: August 25, 1530

Died: March 28, 1584

Birthplace: Kolomenskoye near Moscow

Parents: Grand Duke Vasily III of Moscow (1479–1533) and Yelena Glinskaya (ca.1510–1538)

Nationality: Russian

Historical Role: The first czar of Russia

Reign: December 1533–March 1584

Marital Alliances: Anastasia Romanovna (1547); Maria Temryukovna Cherkasskaya (1561); Marfa Vasilyevna Sobakina (1571); Anna Aleskeyevna Koltovskaya (1572); Maria Dolgorukaya (1573); Anna Ivanova Vasilchikova (1575); Vasilisa Ignatyevna Melentyeva (1577); Maria Fyodorovna Nagaya (1581)

Children: By Anastasia Romanovna: Anna Ivanovna (1548–1550), Maria Ivanovna (1551–ca. 1551), Dmitri Ivanovich (1552–1553), Ivan Ivanovich (1554–1581), Eudoxia Ivanovna (1556–1558), Feodor Ivanovich (1557–1598). By Maria Nagaya: Czarevich Dmitri Ivanovich (1582–1591). There may have been others

Hero or Villain: Ivan's reign began well but he declined into villainy

Elizabeth Báthory, the Blood Countess

KNOWN AS THE "BLOOD COUNTESS" BECAUSE SHE IS ALLEGED TO HAVE REVELLED IN SADISM AND TO HAVE BATHED IN THE BLOOD OF VIRGIN GIRLS IN ORDER TO KEEP HER YOUTH, ELIZABETH BÁTHORY JOINS VLAD THE IMPALER IN NOTORIETY.

Elizabeth Báthory was born in 1560. She grew up on her aristocratic family's estate in Transylvania (birthplace of both Vlad and the fictional Dracula), which was incorporated into the kingdom of Hungary. As a child, she had a series of seizures and often had uncontrollable rages. Her cousin Stephen Báthory, by contrast, became a regional hero, fighting against the Ottoman Empire and against Ivan the Terrible in the Livonian War. Elizabeth, even after her childhood troubles had passed, was to show no such valor.

When she was 14 she was betrothed to Count Ferenc Nádadsy, whom she married in 1575. Given authority over his household at Castle Sárvár, her wickedness began to emerge as she inflicted cruel punishments on servant girls and local peasants. One of her alleged methods of torture was to stick pins under their fingernails. She would also kill some of her victims by stripping them naked, forcing them out into the snow, and dousing them with water so that they would freeze to death. Apparently, her husband Count Nádadsy had a similar penchant for sadism and taught Elizabeth a variation on this punishment that would work in summertime—the naked victim would be covered in honey and tied up outside to become prey for animals and insects.

NOTORIOUS IN HER LIFETIME

Rumors of Elizabeth's murderous activities were already rife by the time of her husband's death in 1604. A Lutheran minister publicly complained about the atrocities, but the stature of the Nádadsy and Báthory families ensured that, to begin with, there was no official inquiry into these vicious crimes. Count Nádadsy himself was a valued commander of

The political divisions in Eastern Europe during the time of the Blood Countess.

The ruins of Elizabeth's castle at Cachtice.

Hungarian forces in the battles against the Ottomans, so officialdom was reluctant to rock the boat.

After the death of Nádadsy, Elizabeth spent most of her time at her castles at Beckov and Cachtice in what is present-day Slovakia, and some of her staff became accomplices to her atrocities. The torture of young servant girls no longer seemed enough—she cast her net wider to attract daughters of the gentry, inviting them into her household. In 1609, one of her victims was a young noblewoman, but this death was harder to cover up than those of servant girls. She claimed that the victim had committed suicide, but an inquiry began to look at the suspicious deaths in her household. This inquiry, which began in 1610, would probably never have happened if there had not been an additional political motivation—Matthias II, the king of Hungary, owed Elizabeth money and sought to wipe out the debt while confiscating Elizabeth's estates.

TALES OF ABDUCTION AND TORTURE

Count György Thurzó, the king's ally, headed the inquiry. The evidence was damning. The body of a dead girl was discovered at Cachtice, while other young women were found dying, wounded, or locked up. He supposedly discovered a diary or register in Elizabeth's own handwriting, giving the details of some 650 victims. As a member of the nobility, Elizabeth was not put on trial, but three of the accomplices who helped administer her cruel deeds were found guilty and sentenced to death.

Some 300 people testified at the inquiry, telling of the murder of adolescent peasant girls and lesser gentry who had come to Cachtice as servants or to learn etiquette. There were tales of abduction, torture, mutilation, and starvation, and that Elizabeth bit her victims while torturing them, leading to accusations of her being a werewolf or vampire. Later, it was claimed that she bathed in the blood of young virgin girls in an attempt to retain her beauty, and that staff at Sárvár Castle had removed over 100 corpses.

BRICKED UP

Elizabeth was placed under house arrest in Cachtice Castle, enduring solitary confinement in a room without windows and with the door bricked up. There was only one air vent and a tiny opening through which her food would be pushed. She died after four years of imprisonment, on August 21, 1614.

The court records of the trials were not released at the time, which gave credence to some of the wilder rumors concerning Elizabeth Báthory. In the early eighteenth century, Jesuit priest Lázló Turóczi investigated the local folklore about her sadism from residents of Cachtice. The stories of her bathing in blood were revealed, and they came to be embellished by further writers and filmmakers, who established her nicknames of the Blood Countess and Countess Dracula.

FACT FILE

Elizabeth Báthory, the Blood Countess

Born: August 7, 1560

Died: August 21, 1614

Birthplace: Nyírbátor, Hungary

Historical Role: Hungarian countess

Marital Alliances: Count Ferenc Nádasdy (1575)

Historic Exploits: Tortured and killed servant girls, peasants, and daughters of the gentry; murdered a young noblewoman at Cachtice Castle in 1609, provoking an official inquiry

Circumstances of Death: Elizabeth was placed under house arrest in Cachtice Castle in 1610. She died after four years of imprisonment

Hero or Villain: Villain

Blackbeard

ONE OF THE MOST NOTORIOUS PIRATES OF THE EIGHTEENTH CENTURY, BLACKBEARD SAILED THE CARIBBEAN AND ATLANTIC COASTS, PURSUING MURDER, MAYHEM, AND TREASURE.

B lackbeard's real name is thought to have been Edward Teach, and he was probably born in Bristol, England, in 1680. Many of his scandalous acts of piracy were sanctioned by the English throne, because he was originally a privateer rather than a pirate. England was at war with Spain in the War of the Spanish Succession (1701–1714), and the conflict spread to the country's rival strongholds in the West Indies, where Teach was based. England sought to weaken Spanish resources by allowing private English sea captains, who were not part of the official navy, to capture and scuttle Spanish ships, and to plunder their cargoes of treasure and merchandise. The major role of the privateers ended at the close of the war, but many of these privateer sea captains and crews became out-and-out pirates, continuing the same policy of capturing ships but without any legal jurisdiction. By 1716,

The Caribbean, where Blackbeard operated in the eighteenth century.

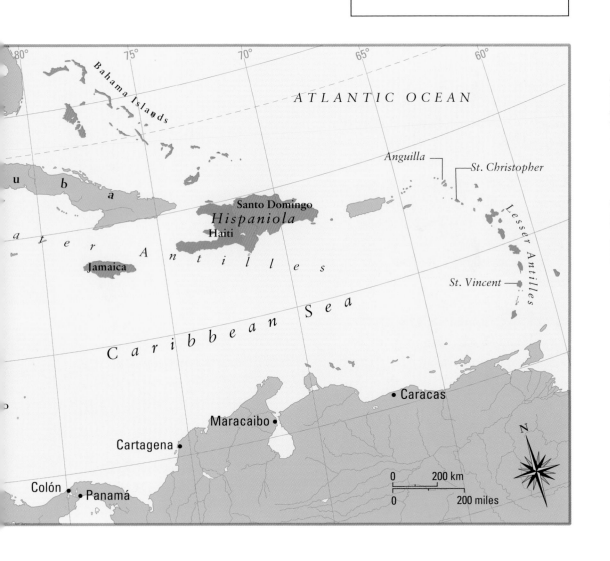

Caribbean Territories
1713

- Spanish Empire
- British possessions
- French possessions

ATLANTIC OCEAN

Bahama Islands

Anguilla — St. Christopher

u b
a

Santo Domingo
Hispaniola
Haiti

a t e r

Jamaica

A n t i l l e s

Lesser Antilles

St. Vincent —

C a r i b b e a n   S e a

• Caracas

Maracaibo •

Cartagena •

Colón •
• Panamá

0   200 km
0   200 miles

N

An eighteenth-century engraving of Blackbeard with his signature black beard arranged in plaits..

it into a warship mounted with 40 guns. He renamed it *Queen Anne's Revenge* after the queen who had ruled England during the War of the Spanish Succession. Meanwhile, Thornigold accepted a pardon for all his misdeeds from the governor of the Bahamas and duly retired as a pirate. Edward Teach was now a pirate captain in his own right.

HUGE BLACK BEARD

Teach's frightening appearance led to the nickname of "Blackbeard." He was tall, with a very loud voice, and had a huge black beard that he twisted into plaits and tied with ribbons. Before attacking a ship, he would dangle cords soaked with saltpeter from his hat and light them so he would be surrounded by black smoke. According to some accounts, he could be merciless, cutting off his victims' fingers to get their rings and sometimes disemboweling them. He is said to have once cut off the ears of a captive and forced him to eat them. His own crew fared little better—he would sometimes randomly fire at them or maroon them if he didn't want to share out his illegal booty.

Teach was serving under the command of the pirate Benjamin Thornigold, and captured cargo that included wine, flour, and gold bullion. Then he attacked and captured a large French merchant ship heading to Martinique. The ship was largely undamaged, so Blackbeard turned

One of Backbeard's greatest escapades was the blockade of Charleston. He would spend the winter in the Caribbean, but in the summer he would base the *Queen Anne's Revenge* and several other stolen vessels in the Ocracoke Inlet on the North Carolina coast, from where he could bully merchant vessels off the coasts of Virginia and Carolina. In May 1718, he took his pirate fleet south to Charleston, South Carolina, and blockaded its harbor, the all-important trading port for the region. Any ship attempting to leave the harbor was attacked, and he took some wealthy citizens as prisoners, whom he agreed to release in return for medical supplies—perhaps an unexpected request for a pirate. When the ransom was met, he stripped the prisoners of their possessions (including their clothes), and deposited them on the shore.

> *Blackbeard's body was thrown into the sea but his head was hung from the bowsprit of Maynard's ship to prove that the infamous pirate was finally dead.*

REWARD DEAD OR ALIVE

He received a pardon from the corrupt governor of North Carolina, who sanctioned his activities as long as he received a share of the spoils. Ships in the local waters became easy prey, so Alexander Spotswood, governor of neighboring Virginia, took it into his own hands to protect trade in the region. He announced a reward for the capture of Blackbeard, dead or alive. Gaining the assistance of the British Navy, in November 1718, Spotswood sent two ships under the command of Lieutenant Robert Maynard to the Ocracoke Inlet to root out the water rat from his nest.

TRICKED ONBOARD

As he approached Blackbeard's ship on November 17, 1718, Maynard's vessels were caught in a shuddering broadside from Blackbeard's guns. Maynard ordered the surviving crew on his main ship to hide below decks, tricking Blackbeard into boarding the vessel in the belief that most of the crew had been killed. They then sprang their ambush. According to Captain Charles Johnson, who wrote a history of great pirates a few years after Blackbeard's death, the pirate "stood his ground and fought with great fury till he received five and twenty wounds." The last blow decapitated him. Blackbeard's body was thrown into the sea. but his head was hung from the bowsprit of Maynard's ship to prove that the infamous pirate was finally dead, and to warn other pirates of their fate. Nonetheless, rumors of his escape continued along with tales of great hoards of buried treasure from his ill-gotten gains. The treasure was never found and probably never existed.

Peter the Great

PETER I BECAME CZAR OF RUSSIA AT NINE AND WOULD BECOME THE MOST INFLUENTIAL LEADER IN THE HISTORY OF HIS COUNTRY UNTIL THE RISE OF COMMUNISM IN THE TWENTIETH CENTURY. THIS WAS NO EASY FEAT.

Remodeling a normal-size country would be a huge achievement, but Peter undertook the complete overhaul of the largest country in the world. Born in 1672, he took on the full responsibilities of government when he was 17, but continued to find himself subjected to the machinations of rivals, regents, and family members. Several members of his own family were killed, and Peter became all too aware of the chaos of disparate forces and the murderous power struggles that were crippling the advancement of Russia.

The years of youthful preparation stood him in good stead for the rest of his life, in which he would transform Russia into an organized empire that would dominate Eastern Europe and become a major Western power. Unlike Ivan the Terrible, who first initiated the empire, Peter I was to be known as a wise and largely beneficent ruler, who remains a hero to many in Russia today, and who is usually referred to as "Peter the Great."

Peter was both an intellectual and physical giant—he was over 6 ft 6 in (1.9 m) tall. He was fiercely determined to change radically the Eastern perspective that he felt was holding Russia back. To do this, he weakened the power of the highly influential Orthodox Church and forbade any man to become a priest until the age of 50. As few people lived to that age, the effect on the Church was catastrophic. Instead, Peter looked toward the best of Western systems in his attempts to push forward the political and civic administration and culture of Mother Russia.

"ORDER AND DEFENSE"

As Peter wrote to his son Alexis in 1715: "Two things are necessary in government— order and defense." In 1696, he scored a significant victory against the Ottoman empire, the main power base in both Eastern Europe and along the southwestern borders of Russia. Despite this victory, Peter knew that both the Ottomans and the Swedes, who had spread from Scandinavia, would continually threaten Russia with invasion unless he reorganized the country's defenses and secured European allies. Setting off in 1697, he toured Europe for 18 months. Although he failed to encourage France and Austria to join him against the Ottomans, he was greeted with greater warmth in Holland and Britain.

There, he was able to study Western administrations at first hand and left no stone unturned in his pursuit of knowledge. He even worked in the Dutch shipyards for four months so that he could learn more about the skills and materials required to build a stronger fleet; he then went to Manchester to look at how a city could be built rapidly. On his return, he totally modernized the army, extended his fleet, remodeled the legal and administrative systems, and brought the importance of education to the fore. He also tried to put an end to arranged marriages (his own first marriage, arranged by his mother, was a deeply unhappy one) and changed the Russian calendar to match that of the West.

WAR WITH SWEDEN

For both trade and military purposes, he needed a stretch of coast with access to the main body of Europe, so he undertook a long and difficult war with Sweden in 1700–1721, resulting in him securing parts of Latvia and Finland and the whole of Estonia.

This included a large stretch of the Baltic coastline, effectively opening up greater trade between Russia and the great Western powers. In 1712, this westward expansion also allowed him to establish a new capital at St. Petersburg, significantly nearer the West that he was trying to emulate than the traditional capital of Moscow. Construction of St. Petersburg began in 1703, and the city had already become a fulcrum for the arts by the time of Peter's death. The campaign against the Swedes was immediately followed by a war with Persia, in which Russia acquired Baku, a city-port on the Caspian Sea (situated in modern-day Azerbaijan).

RUTHLESS STREAK

Peter did not achieve all this without a ruthless streak or setbacks. He forced his first wife to become a nun to be free of her, and allowed his own son to be tortured to death following accusations of plotting. He had 1,200 rebels tortured and executed when they attempted a mutiny in 1698. Furthermore, he was never able to defeat the Ottomans, who continued to trouble his southern borders and in 1710 forced him to hand back ports on the Black Sea. However, by the time he died in 1725, he had changed Russia forever. Despite all his other achievements, St. Petersburg is the jewel in his crown and to this day, remains one of the world's most beautiful and great cities.

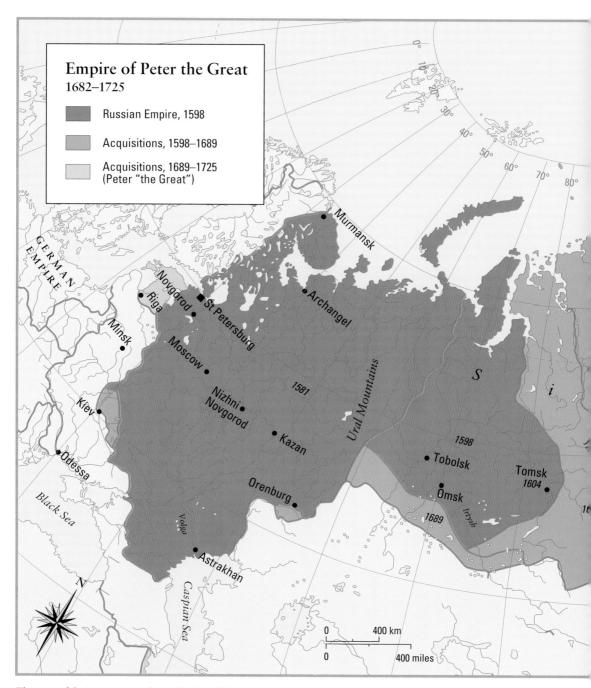

The extent of the Russian empire during the reign of Peter the Great.

180°
70°
60°
Anadyr
1762
1800
170°
160°
150°
140°
130°
120°
110°
Nizhni Kolymsk
1644
a
Nizhni
Kamchatsk
50°
i
Okhotsk
1648
Sea
of
Okhotsk
Petropavlovsk
r
Yakutsk
1632
Lena
e
Yeniseysk
1619
Amur Region
1650–1689
to China 1689
R. Amur
U s s u r i
Chita
Irkutsk
1652
40°
M a n c h u r i a
Urga
Sea
of
Japan
M o n g o l i a
CHINA
J A P A N
Tokyo

George Washington

COMMANDER OF THE AMERICAN REVOLUTIONARY FORCES, THE FIRST PRESIDENT OF THE UNITED STATES, AND THE FATHER OF HIS COUNTRY—QUITE AN ACHIEVEMENT FOR A SELF-TAUGHT LAND SURVEYOR.

Washington was born in Pope's Creek, Virginia, in 1732, the great-grandchild of John Washington, an Englishman who had migrated to North America 75 years earlier. George was set for a career as a land surveyor when his brother died, leaving him his Mount Vernon estate and allowing him to become a member of the country gentry. He was no idle young gentleman, however, and soon became the lieutenant-general of the Virginia military. He succeeded in driving the French out of Fort Duquesne in 1754, but then suffered his first military setback when he had to surrender Fort Necessity.

He resigned his command when he married wealthy widow Martha Custis in 1758 and became involved in politics. He had a particular interest in disputes between the American colonies and their ruler, the British Crown; he was elected as a delegate to the first and second Continental Congresses, which represented the interests of the colonies, in 1774–1775. The British government had provoked the Americans with a series of unfair taxes and the denial of their full rights as citizens, but thought that it could subdue the colonials by its military presence. It was wrong. Washington could see that war was inevitable and had already started supplying Virginia with arms and training soldiers by the time of the second Congress. Washington was given command of the colonial armies on June 15, 1775, shortly after the American War of Independence began. The second Continental Congress made a Declaration of Independence on behalf of the thirteen American colonies in July 1776, rejecting the authority of the British monarchy.

Commander-in-chief Washington continually battled against the odds: his troops often had shortages of arms and supplies and were given very little training;

The fall of Yorktown and Cornwallis' surrender.

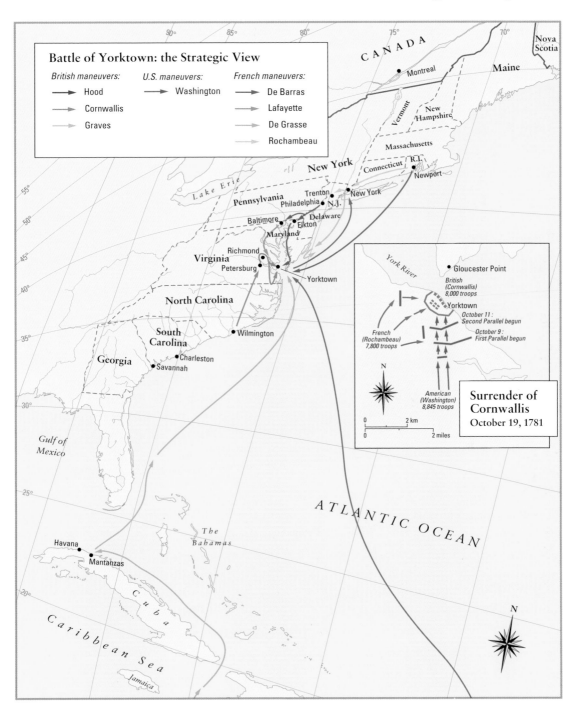

Battle of Yorktown: the Strategic View

British maneuvers:
→ Hood
→ Cornwallis
→ Graves

U.S. maneuvers:
→ Washington

French maneuvers:
→ De Barras
→ Lafayette
→ De Grasse
→ Rochambeau

Surrender of Cornwallis
October 19, 1781

York River

• Gloucester Point

British (Cornwallis) 8,000 troops

Yorktown

October 11: Second Parallel begun

October 9: First Parallel begun

French (Rochambeau) 7,800 troops

American (Washington) 8,845 troops

0   2 km
0   2 miles

CANADA

Nova Scotia

Maine

Montreal

Vermont

New Hampshire

Massachusetts

New York

Connecticut

R.I.

Newport

Lake Erie

Pennsylvania

Trenton

N.J.

Philadelphia

New York

Delaware

Baltimore

Elkton

Maryland

Richmond

Virginia

Petersburg

Yorktown

North Carolina

South Carolina

Wilmington

Georgia

Charleston

Savannah

Gulf of Mexico

The Bahamas

ATLANTIC OCEAN

Havana

Mantanzas

Cuba

Caribbean Sea

Jamaica

N

and his generals indulged themselves with in-fighting. By contrast, the British had a fully equipped, well-organized professional army. Despite the disparities, Washington had notable victories at Boston, Trenton, and Princeton, although he was defeated at Brooklyn Heights and, in 1777, Brandywine and Germantown. Fortunately, the French joined the war on the side of the Americans, and the British gave up Philadelphia in order to set up a military stronghold at New York. After harassing the British troops at the Battle of Monmouth on their way to New York, Washington bided his time.

He wasn't the author of the Constitution, but he did a great deal to remove the obstacles to an agreement. He was unanimously chosen as first president ...

THE FALL OF YORKTOWN

In 1781, he saw his opportunity when British commander Lord Cornwallis, had defeats in North Carolina and withdrew to Yorktown on the coast of Virginia. Washington's army and a French force united north of New York and hurried southward, picking up reinforcements along the way to form an army of about 19,000 men. In the meantime, the French fleet defeated the British Navy, leaving New York and Yorktown as the only British strongholds. Washington surrounded Yorktown, and Cornwallis was forced to draw back from his outer defenses, hoping to sit tight until a promised relief force of 5,000 arrived. The relief came too late. On October 9, the allies opened fire with their heavy artillery and bombarded the British; on October 14, Washington sent the soldiers into battle, and they made great headway. Cornwallis, facing defeat, attempted to evacuate his troops across the York river but the weather made this impossible. On October 19, 1781, the British surrendered. The Treaty of Paris, officially ending the war, would not be signed for two years, but the war was effectively concluded that day in Yorktown. The Colonies were free.

FIRST PRESIDENT

Washington's personal fortune had been largely destroyed by the conflict. Following the Treaty of Paris, he returned to Virginia to manage his estates. He stayed there for four years until, in 1787, he was chosen to join the Virginia delegation to write the U.S. Constitution. Now Washington's diplomatic skills came to the fore. He wasn't the author of the Constitution, but he did a great deal to remove obstacles to an agreement. He was then unanimously chosen as the first

However, his pragmatic policies enabled the economy of the new nation to find a sound footing through the reestablishment of trade with the old country. In 1797, he turned down the opportunity of a third term in office and was finally allowed to retire to his estates, having used his considerable military and political aptitude to help create an independent and democratic nation. He died in 1799.

George Washington is captured in a painting by Rembrandt Peale (ca. 1850)

president of the United States of America, and inaugurated on April 30, 1789.

To some extent, Washington was a reluctant politician. He wanted to retire at the end of his first term, but fellow politicians convinced him to stay on. He was again elected by unanimous vote. He was accused of appeasement by his critics, who saw his neutral policy regarding the French Revolution and his resolution of differences with Britain as weaknesses.

FACT FILE

George Washington

Born: February 22, 1732

Died: December 14, 1799

Birthplace: Pope's Creek, Virginia

Historical Role: First president of the United States and key player in the American War of Independence

Presidency: April 1789–March 1797

Marital Alliances: Married Martha Dandridge Custis Washington in 1758

Historical Feats: Led American forces to victory in the American Revolutionary War; oversaw the writing of the American Constitution; became the first president of the United States

Hero or Villain: Hero of American independence

Maximilien Robespierre

HERO OF THE FRENCH REVOLUTION, MAXIMILIEN ROBESPIERRE INFLICTED A TERRIFYING VERSION OF ABSOLUTE RULE IN THE REIGN OF TERROR AS HE SENT MANY CITIZENS TO THE GUILLOTINE, BUT HE SOON MET HIS OWN END IN THE SAME WAY.

Maximilien François-Marie Isidore de Robespierre was born in Arras, France, in May 1758. A lawyer who rose to prominence in the French Revolution, he was elected to the National Assembly in 1789. He became extremely popular in Paris, where he emerged as an enemy of monarchy and defender of the rights of citizens. He appeared to be so disinterested in the trappings of power that he earned the epithet of "the Incorruptible." He became the leader of the left-wing Jacobins in the National Convention, which abolished the monarchy, put the deposed monarch Louis XVI on trial for treason, and declared France a republic on September 21, 1792.

Robespierre called for the execution of Louis. This was in contrast to the ruling Girondists, the right-wing republicans who preferred a lesser punishment for the former king. Robespierre won the day and Louis was executed by guillotine in January 1793 in the Place de la Révolution (a square in Paris that had previously been named Place Louis XV after the king's father and is now Place de la Concorde). The beheading took place with the fervent support of most of the populace. The Jacobins used this wave of popular support to mount a coup against the Girondists, declaring them to be counterrevolutionary "corrupt deputies," and had their leaders arrested. Support for the Jacobins was such that revolutionary committees started to replace or share power with town councils across France.

CHAOS REIGNS

France was in chaos and facing the possibility of both civil war and foreign invasion led by other monarchs and antirepublican interests in Europe. In response, the Jacobins set up the Committee of Public Safety—a somewhat mundane title for the small body of men who now

The centers of conflict during the French Revolution.

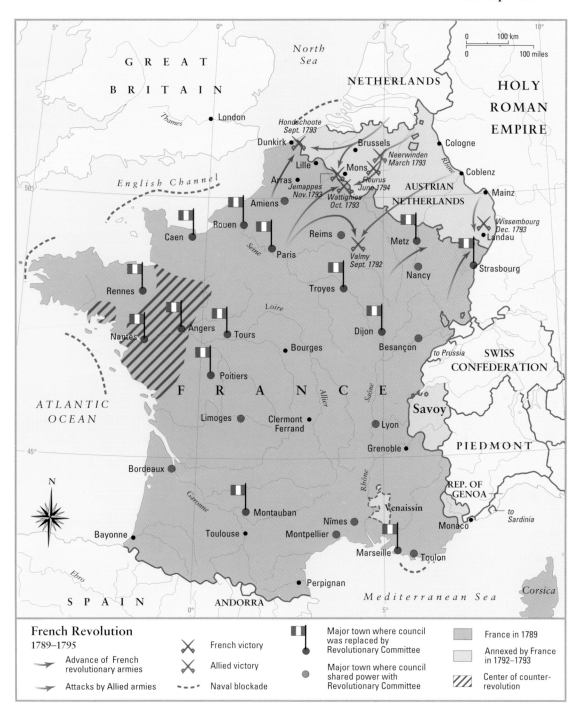

French Revolution
1789–1795

→ Advance of French revolutionary armies

→ Attacks by Allied armies

✕ French victory

✕ Allied victory

- - - Naval blockade

⚑ Major town where council was replaced by Revolutionary Committee

● Major town where council shared power with Revolutionary Committee

France in 1789

Annexed by France in 1792–1793

Center of counter-revolution

effectively ruled France. Robespierre was appointed a member in July 1793. Very quickly, he began to dominate the committee, even though he was just 35. He removed his rivals, placed his own supporters in all the positions of power, and took control of the Revolutionary Tribunal. All the checks and balances that had been put in place to stop a single man ever gaining absolute power in France again had been swept aside. As his power increased, his popularity with the masses waned; he showed himself to be too much of an autocratic zealot for most people's taste.

TERROR AS OFFICIAL POLICY

Under Robespierre, France endured a Reign of Terror. In September 1793, the Convention issued a decree that it was "time to horrify all the conspirators. So, legislators place Terror on the order of the day...The blade of the law should hover over all the guilty." With Robespierre claiming that "Terror is nothing else than justice," terror was now official policy. His Revolutionary Tribunal began an intense, frenzied and merciless campaign against antirevolutionaries, accusing them of vague "crimes against liberty" on the flimsiest of evidence.

The guillotine became the symbol of the time—more than 16,000 people in France lost their lives to its blade, while another

A portrait of Robespierre (ca. 1790) by an anonymous artist.

25,000 were executed by other means. No element of society was spared. Royals, aristocrats, Girondists, clergymen, farmers, peasants, and even former instigators of the Revolution were all slain on charges that ranged from antirepublicanism to hoarding food stores, and desertion from the army. In April 1794, even Georges Danton, a hero of the Revolution, a former friend of Robespierre, and a moderate Jacobin, was sent to the guillotine as a result of ambiguous evidence. No one in France was safe from the attentions of bloodthirsty Madame Guillotine.

DOWNFALL OF A REVOLUTIONARY

In May 1794, Robespierre, his ego unrestrained, proclaimed a new official religion for the nation—the Cult of the Supreme Being—according to the tenets of his own personal belief in God. His fellow revolutionaries were not amused, especially as Robespierre seemed to take the opportunity of the festival that inaugurated the religion to appear as some sort of absolute divine ruler. His supporters had even gone so far as to demand that Robespierre should be officially appointed the dictator of France.

By this time, he had made too many enemies on both the left and the right, and his popular support had largely evaporated. Robespierre was now portrayed as a power-hungry fanatic who would slay his enemies with little rhyme or reason. The people who perpetrated the Reign of Terror themselves turned against him. Robespierre fled, and was arrested in the course of a struggle. He was shot in the jaw during the fracas, either in a botched suicide attempt or by an assailant. On the next day, July 28, 1794, Robespierre himself was led to the guillotine, along with twenty-one of his leading supporters.

FACT FILE

Maximilien Robespierre

Born: May 6, 1758

Died: July 28, 1794

Birthplace: Arras, France

Nationality: French

Parents: Maximilien Barthélémy François de Robespierre (1732–1777) and Jacqueline Marguerite Carrault (1735–1764)

Historical Role: Leader of the left-wing Jacobins and a key player in the French Revolution

Historic Feats: Declared France to be a republic on September 21, 1792; dominated the Committee of Public Safety and took control of the Revolutionary Tribunal; decreed the Reign of Terror in 1793

Hero or Villain: Began as a supposedly "incorruptible" hero but was later deemed villainous

Royals, aristocrats, Girondists, clergymen, farmers, peasants, and even former instigators of the Revolution were all slain on charges that ranged from anti-republicanism to hoarding food stores, and desertion from the army.

CA SER

AnD 1492 a Christophoro Columbo nomine Regis
Castellæ primum detecta & ab Americo Vespu-
cio nomen sortita 1499

NOVA
GRANADA

Sinus Mexicanus

R

DEL

ZUR Hilpanis

AEQUINOCTIALIS LINEA

SALOMONIS

INSULA

MARE PACI

TROPICUS CAPRICORNI

SICUM

AMERICANA MEXICANA

NINETEENTH CENTURY

The great heroes and villains of the nineteenth century, almost without exception, made their reputations through great campaigns and battles, some military and some political, all significant to the course of history. Admiral Nelson, Napoleon, the Duke of Wellington, Bolivar, Lincoln, and Bismarck were giant figures on the historical stage, each involved in great conflicts in their times. Both Wilburforce and Florence Nightingale were tireless campaigners in the fight to abolish slavery and improve medical treatment on the battlefield respectively. Cecil Rhodes was a businessman and politician whose influence changed the map of Africa, while the legend of Australian criminal Ned Kelly lives on in that country's historical psyche.

Horatio Nelson

BLINDED IN ONE EYE, THEN LOSING HIS RIGHT ARM IN 1797, SOME MAY HAVE QUESTIONED NELSON'S ABILITY TO EVEN COMMAND A SHIP. YET AT TRAFALGAR, HIS BRILLIANCE MADE HIM A BRITISH NATIONAL HERO LONG AFTER HIS DEATH.

Born on September 29, 1758, Nelson joined the crew of a ship commanded by his uncle in 1771. When he joined the navy at 12, he probably never dreamed that one day he would be the most famous admiral in British history. He was a captain by the time he was 20, and served in the West Indies, North America, and the Baltic. Marriage and several frustrating years of inaction followed as he awaited the command of a ship.

His chance came with the advent of the Revolutionary Wars with France in 1793, and he was given the command of HMS *Agamemnon*. He would hardly step foot on dry land for the next seven years. His animosity toward the French during both the Revolutionary and Napoleonic wars was intense, once saying to a crewman, "You must hate a Frenchman as you hate the devil," but he made decisions that were clear-headed as well as bold and decisive. He helped capture Corsica in 1794, losing his eye in the process. It was not only this supposedly incapacitating injury that spurred on his detractors—his unconventional strategies would often lead him to defy orders while in pursuit of victory. Such defiance led to the defeat of the Spanish at Cape Vincent in 1797, where he ignored orders. Again he ignored orders at Copenhagen in 1801; he defeated the Danish after placing his telescope to his blind eye and thereby claiming that he could not see his commander's signal to withdraw.

He suffered further injury during the Battle of Santa Cruz de Tenerife against the Spanish in 1797, when he was hit by a musketball. He instructed the ship's surgeon to amputate his severely damaged arm, and resumed command just 30 minutes later. Whatever his injuries, his capabilities could not be ignored—especially considering he all but destroyed Napoleon's fleet at the Battle of the Nile just a year later.

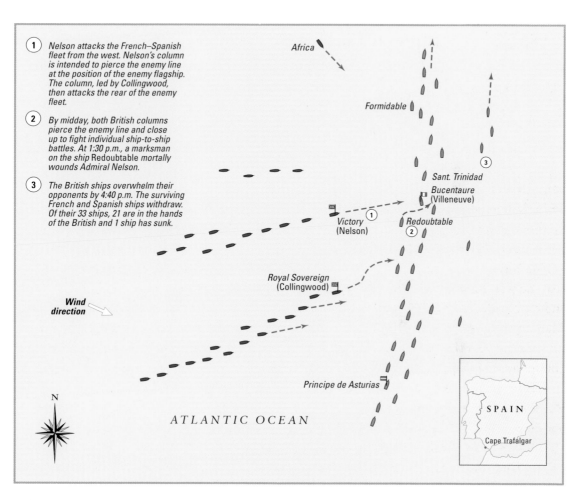

1. Nelson attacks the French–Spanish fleet from the west. Nelson's column is intended to pierce the enemy line at the position of the enemy flagship. The column, led by Collingwood, then attacks the rear of the enemy fleet.

2. By midday, both British columns pierce the enemy line and close up to fight individual ship-to-ship battles. At 1:30 p.m., a marksman on the ship Redoubtable mortally wounds Admiral Nelson.

3. The British ships overwhelm their opponents by 4:40 p.m. The surviving French and Spanish ships withdraw. Of their 33 ships, 21 are in the hands of the British and 1 ship has sunk.

Africa

Formidable

Sant. Trinidad

Bucentaure (Villeneuve)

Victory (Nelson)

Redoubtable

Royal Sovereign (Collingwood)

Wind direction

Principe de Asturias

ATLANTIC OCEAN

N

SPAIN

Cape Trafálgar

Nelson's successful strategy at the Battle of Trafalgar.

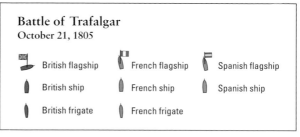

Battle of Trafalgar
October 21, 1805

British flagship   French flagship   Spanish flagship

British ship   French ship   Spanish ship

British frigate   French frigate

THE LADY HAMILTON AFFAIR

It was not only Nelson's actions at sea that ruffled feathers. In 1800, while in Naples, his reputation was threatened when he began an affair with Lady Hamilton, although they were both married at the time. He returned to England and separated from his wife, and had a daughter called Horatia with Lady Hamilton a year later. Despite his injuries and scandalous lovelife, he maintained much support in the Admiralty, where he was acknowledged as a great naval tactician and leader of men. He was promoted to vice-admiral in 1801 and, after the success in Copenhagen, turned his attention back to the Mediterranean in order to lead the navy's ongoing sea battles against France and its Spanish allies.

He blockaded their fleets in Toulon for two years, but his wily French adversary, Pierre-Charles Villeneuve (Napoleon's admiral), escaped the blockade in 1805. Nelson chased him all the way to the West Indies and back again, but failed to secure a full-on confrontation with his fleet.

His chance finally came when the combined French and Spanish fleets left the port of Cádiz in southern Spain.

Napoleon Bonaparte was planning an invasion of England and there would no greater test of Nelson's capabilities than to destroy this threat. Before the battle off Cape Trafalgar on October 21, 1805, the admiral went below decks on HMS *Victory* to make out his will and then sent a message to his fleet: "England expects that every man will do his duty." And they did just that. Nelson knew that the enemy fleet of 33 ships would form a traditional line of battle, in which the fleet would be spread out nose-to-tail in a long line. Consequently, he split up his own smaller fleet of 27 ships—leading one section himself, with Admiral Collingwood heading a second squadron. The squadrons then attacked the Franco-Spanish line at different points, severing it and making it impossible for Villeneuve to control his fleet. During the battle, 21 enemy ships were captured and one ship was sunk, while not a single British ship was lost in what proved to be the most impressive naval victory in British history.

> *Nelson ... then sent a message to his fleet: "England expects that every man will do his duty." And they did just that.*

"KISS ME, HARDY"

However, this time Nelson was mortally wounded and was unable to defy death yet again. In a fierce exchange with a French

An engraving of Admiral Horatio Nelson.

ship, the *Redoubtable*, Nelson had been shot through the spine by a sniper. He is alleged to have died in the arms of the captain of the *Victory*, asking him to look after Lady Hamilton and saying, "Kiss me, Hardy." His crew preserved his body in a barrel of brandy and sailed homeward. Despite the complete destruction of the threat of invasion by Napoleon, King George III is alleged to have responded to the news of Nelson's death with the words, "We have lost more than we have gained." To this day, his reputation is undiminished, and his statue at the top of Nelson's Column dominates London's Trafalgar Square.

FACT FILE

Horatio Nelson

Born: September 29, 1758

Died: October 21, 1805

Birthplace: Burnham Thorpe, Norfolk

Historical Role: British Naval Commander (1771–1805)

Marital Alliances: Francis Nisbet (1787) and Emma, Lady Hamilton (1791)

Children: By Lady Hamilton: Horatia Nelson (1801–1881)

Historic Feats: Nelson helped capture Corsica (1794); the battle at Cape Vincent (1797); the Battle of the Nile (1798); blockade of French and Spanish fleets at Toulon; the battle off Cape Trafalgar (1805)

Legacy: Nelson's victory at the Battle of Trafalgar prevented Napoleon Bonaparte from invading Britain

Hero or Villain: British Naval hero

William Wilberforce

IN HIS DIARY, WILBERFORCE WROTE "GOD ALMIGHTY HAS SET BEFORE ME TWO GREAT OBJECTS, THE SUPPRESSION OF THE SLAVE TRADE AND THE REFORMATION OF MANNERS." HE DIED WITHIN THREE DAYS OF SLAVERY'S ABOLITION IN BRITAIN.

Born in Hull in the north of England on August 24, 1759, William Wilberforce was the son of a wealthy merchant. He studied at Oxford University, where he had the good fortune to become friends with William Pitt the Younger, the future prime minister of Britain. Wilberforce was more concerned with the pursuit of his own pleasures—especially drinking and gambling—than considering the plight of millions of slaves across the world. He was originally thought, even by members of his own family and political sympathizers, to be lazy and morally destitute, but he turned out to be a tireless campaigner and a man of extraordinary willpower.

EVANGELICAL CONVERSION

This tiny, frail man—he was barely over 5 ft (1.5 m) tall—became a Member of Parliament for his home town in 1780 at the age of just 21. During the course of the next ten years, his personality changed radically and he became an evangelical Christian. He formed a close association with Thomas Clarkson and the Clapham Sect, an Anglican religious group that fervently campaigned through books, pamphlets, and rallies for the abolition of the slave trade. Along with several prominent Quakers, they created the Society for Effecting the Abolition of the Slave Trade, and adopted the well-known potter Josiah Wedgwood's motif of a kneeling slave in chains imploring "Am I Not a Man and a Brother?"

British ships were responsible for transporting, in awful conditions, millions of slaves from Africa to the West Indies and to parts of North America. Here, they would be sold like merchandise in return for slave-grown produce, such as cotton and tobacco, which would be shipped back to Britain. As one observer commented, the slaves were stowed in the ships' holds like "herrings in a barrel." Disease would

Routes of the slave trade.

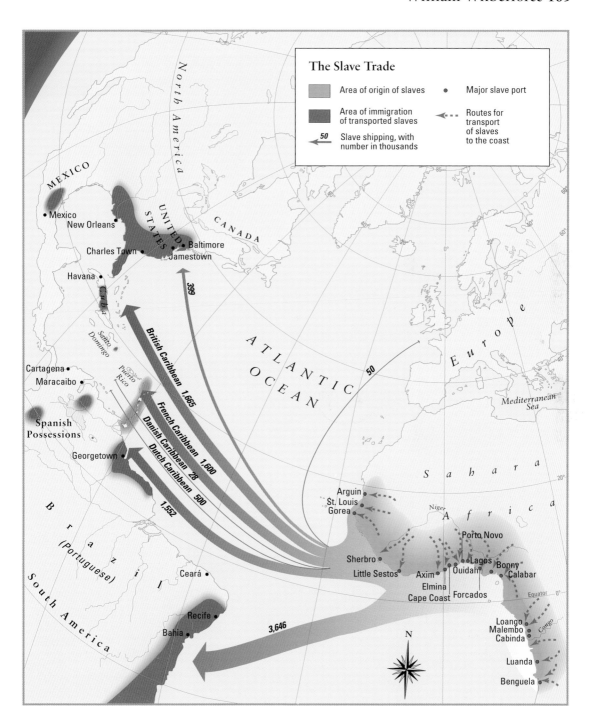

The Slave Trade

- Area of origin of slaves
- Area of immigration of transported slaves
- → 50 Slave shipping, with number in thousands
- ● Major slave port
- ◄┈┈ Routes for transport of slaves to the coast

Diagram of a slave ship

STOWAGE OF THE BRITISH SLAVE SHIP "BROOKES" UNDER THE
REGULATED SLAVE TRADE
Act of 1788.

be rampant in the ships' dungeon-like quarters, and many would die before the end of their voyage from Africa. More than ten million Africans were transported into slavery, with over a million dying en route. This grim trade was responsible for over three quarters of Britain's foreign income, so powerful forces lobbied for it and stood in the way of its abolition. Wilberforce became the voice of the abolitionists in parliament. He began to introduce antislavery motions in the House of Commons, where he had the support of Pitt the Younger until the latter's premature death in 1806. Wilberforce's greatest achievement came in 1807, when a bill for the abolition of the slave trade, which had the support of the new Prime Minister Lord Grenville, became law. British ships would no longer be allowed to transport slaves, and captains would be fined a huge sum of £100 for every slave found onboard. However, captains who persisted in the trade would simply throw slaves overboard if they were pursued by Royal Navy ships.

The monumental job of wiping out all slavery was still only half done. It may have become illegal to trade in slaves, but it was still possible to own them; there were millions of people still trapped in slavery across the colonies of the British Empire. Wilberforce, as his detractors point out, was not keen on immediate emancipation for those who were already slaves—he preferred "gradual abolition," as he thought they needed to be "trained and educated for freedom." In the end, he did join the campaign for the complete emancipation of existing slaves but, because of failing health, he retired from parliament in 1825 and it was left to others to complete his work. Nonetheless, it was largely due to his efforts that slavery was completely abolished in most of the British Empire in 1833. Slavery would persist in the U.S. for many years

Wilberforce also helped to establish Sierra Leone in Africa as a slavery-free area prior to the abolition of slavery

elsewhere. In 1833, Wilberforce caught influenza from which he never recovered. On July 26, he was assured that the Slavery Abolition Act would be passed in parliament and three days later he died, his life's work complete. He was buried near Pitt the Younger in Westminster Abbey and is still revered throughout the world for his role as a tireless campaigner against slavery.

FACT FILE

William Wilberforce

Born: August 24, 1759

Died: July 29, 1833

Birthplace: Hull, England

Historical Role: Politician and key player in the abolition of the slave trade in the British Empire

Marital Alliances: Barbara Spooner (1797)

Historic Feats: Wilberforce's bill for the abolition of the slave trade became law in 1807

Legacy: Wilberforce became a member of parliament for his home town at the age of just 21, and his work set Britain on the path toward the abolition of slavery in 1833

Hero or Villain: Abolitionist hero

Napoleon Bonaparte

TO ALL APPEARANCES, NAPOLEON WAS A SUPPORTER OF THE FRENCH REVOLUTION, AND HE ROSE TO PROMINENCE IN THE REVOLUTIONARY WARS IN 1795. HOWEVER, THE MOTTO OF THE REVOLUTION WAS A FAR CRY FROM HIS REAL INTENTIONS.

Within four years, he would declare himself dictator of France and his ambitions did not rest with that achievement—he wanted the whole of Europe. A gentrified but rough-hewn man of small stature, Napoleon was born in Corsica in 1769 and joined the French army at the age of 16. He suppressed a royalist uprising in Paris in 1795 on behalf of the Revolution, and was made a general, leading the French to victories against the Austrians. He then conquered Egypt in order to damage Britain's all-important trade routes with India, and invaded Syria.

However, in 1798 he came up against his naval nemesis, Horatio Nelson, who destroyed his fleet in the Battle of the Nile. Napoleon took the failure in his stride, and returned to France to seize power from the government and set himself up as a dictator. The French, who had done so much to overthrow their monarch and aristocracy just a few years earlier, took this despotic man to their bosoms, voting to make him consul for life in 1802 and emperor in 1804.

EUROPEAN AMBITIONS

Absolute power in France was not enough for Napoleon. He started his campaign to seize Europe in 1803, provoking Britain and its allies, Austria, Prussia, and Russia, into entering the Napoleonic Wars. Only Nelson's endeavors at the Battle of Trafalgar in 1805, when the French and Spanish fleets were captured, prevented him invading England.

Napoleon's military genius came to the fore at Austerlitz, in December of that year, when he defeated the Austrian Empire. He tempted the combined forces of the Russian Czar Alexander I and the Austrian Holy Roman Emperor Francis II to attack his left flank by deliberately weakening it, before launching his own attack from

Tactics employed by Napoleon at the Battle of Austerlitz.

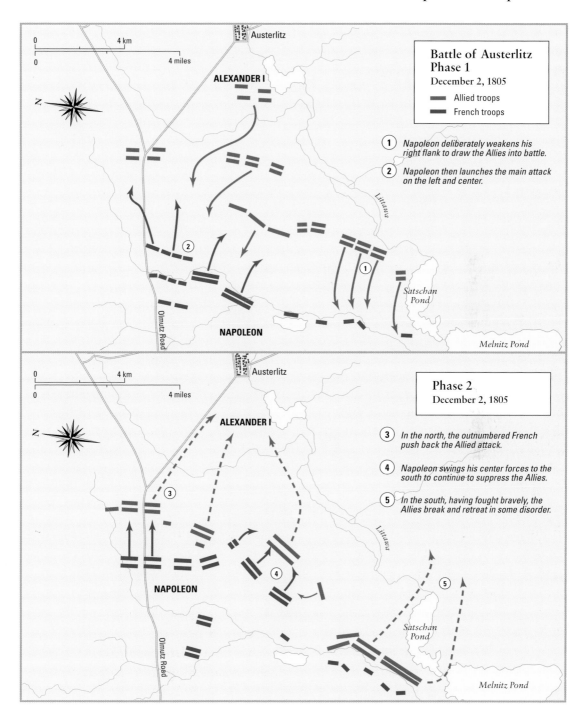

**Battle of Austerlitz
Phase 1**
December 2, 1805

━━ Allied troops
━━ French troops

(1) Napoleon deliberately weakens his
right flank to draw the Allies into battle.

(2) Napoleon then launches the main attack
on the left and center.

Phase 2
December 2, 1805

(3) In the north, the outnumbered French
push back the Allied attack.

(4) Napoleon swings his center forces to the
south to continue to suppress the Allies.

(5) In the south, having fought bravely, the
Allies break and retreat in some disorder.

An early engraving of Napoleon in characteristic pose.

the center and left. There were more than 150,000 soldiers and cavalry embroiled in a monumental struggle on the battlefield, but Napoleon's maneuver won the day.

Within a few months, the Holy Roman Empire—the mainstay of power throughout a swathe of Europe for centuries—was no more. In the following years, Prussia was defeated and Russia was forced into an alliance with Napoleon. The whole of Europe was Napoleon's for the taking, and he installed his brothers and loyalists as puppet kings across Europe, including Spain and Italy, while cutting off

British trade with the Continent. However, Britain continued to be the thorn in his side, aiding revolts against French control. The British campaign in the Peninsular War from 1808 was led by Arthur Wellesley, the future Duke of Wellington, who secured Portugal as a base from which to attack the French in Spain, while the Spanish themselves conducted one of the first large-scale guerrilla campaigns (*guerrilla* means "little war" in Spanish) against their former allies.

When Napoleon discovered that Russia was also persisting in its alliance with Britain, he made the error of marching toward Moscow in 1812—exactly the same mistake that another egomaniacal tyrant, Adolf Hitler, would make in World War II. Napoleon could not take Moscow and he made a disastrous retreat, his forces decimated by the harsh Russian winter and the destruction of his vital supply lines.

EXILE ON ELBA

The Austrian and Prussian allies regained their nerve, driving the weakened French from Germany and even taking Paris. Napoleon was made to abdicate in 1814 and exiled to the island of Elba, 12 miles (19 km) off the coast of Tuscany. However, he soon escaped, to the horror of Britain and mainland Europe. He reassumed power in France in May 1815, but the Prussians and British, under the leadership of the Duke of Wellington, crushed him at the Battle of Waterloo in June. He surrendered to the British and abdicated once again. This time he was exiled to the arid island of St. Helena, more than 1,000 miles(1,600 km) from the west coast of Africa. This time he could not escape, and he died there on May 5, 1821. His death gave rise to a certain amount of controversy—some believed that he had been poisoned by his British captors, while a diagnosis of cancer was also mooted as the cause of death.

Napoleon was a bullying power monger whose self-belief knew no bounds and led to the deaths of tens of thousands. Yet there is no disputing that he was a political, military, and administrative genius. He managed to convince the French nation, which had only just thrown off the tyranny of the monarchs, to support his endeavors and, in return, he made many laws and administrative reforms that still survive effectively in France. If he had stopped provoking the British, and if he had not attempted his foolhardy Russian campaign, mainland Europe would be a very different place today.

Duke of Wellington

OFTEN ACCLAIMED AS BRITAIN'S GREATEST MILITARY LEADER, THE DUKE OF WELLINGTON'S INCREDIBLE MILITARY ACHIEVEMENTS, NOT HIS POLITICAL CAREER, HAVE MADE HIM A BELOVED NATIONAL BRITISH HERO.

This great British hero was actually born in Ireland as Arthur Wesley (he changed the spelling to Wellesley) in 1769. The son of a wealthy Anglo-Irish peer, he was educated at Eton before serving in the British Army in Flanders and then, from 1796, in India. He achieved remarkable victories on behalf of Britain's imperial interests in the Mysore War and at Assaye in 1803. He earned a knighthood as a result, and on returning to England, became a member of parliament.

He briefly became chief secretary for Ireland in 1807, but soon returned to active service. He established himself as a major national hero for his endeavors in the Peninsular War against Napoleon in 1808–1814. He commanded allied British and Portuguese forces from his base in Portugal, conducting major forays into Spain to harass the occupying French forces. He finally managed to oust the French from the entire Iberian Peninsula in 1814. When he returned home after the abdication of Napoleon, he was greeted as a hero and given the title of Duke of Wellington. He then attended the Congress of Vienna to help plot the future shape of Europe in the absence of Napoleon.

NAPOLEON'S NEMESIS

Again, his sojourn away from the battlefield would prove to be brief. When Napoleon returned to power in 1815, having escaped from enforced exile, Wellington was deemed to be the best man to lead the allied British, German, Dutch, and Belgian forces, numbering 70,000, against the French dictator. He joined forces with the 50,000-strong Prussian forces commanded by Gebhard von Blücher. They met Napoleon's army at the Battle of Waterloo in Belgium on June 18, 1815. Wellington had never directly fought with Napoleon before and it was to prove the greatest triumph of his career.

Wellington took the west of the huge battlefield with the Prussians belatedly

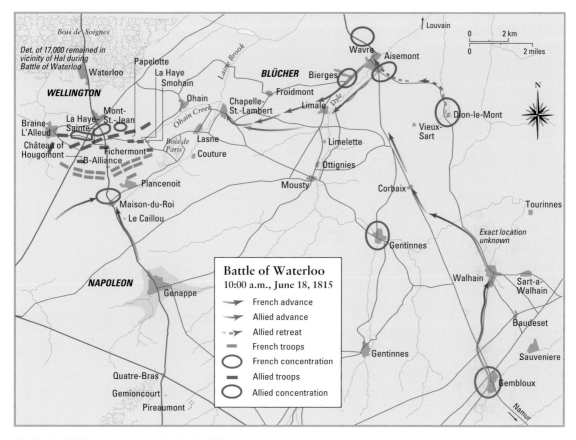

The Duke of Wellington's strategy at the Battle of Waterloo.

arriving to the east. Commanded by General Ney, the French tried to break Wellington's army at the center with his cavalry, but Blücher's capable General Freiherr von Bülow arrived to support Wellington's left flank and the attack was repelled. Ney then made inroads with his artillery, but Wellington skillfully readjusted his line until the Dutch force of William, Prince of Orange, could mount a charge. Meanwhile, British foot soldiers and light infantry to the west slaughtered the cavalry of the esteemed French Old Guard. Wellington pushed forward his forces while the now fully assembled Prussians made advances to the east. As the Guard retreated at full pelt, the remaining French army panicked and abandoned the battlefield. Napoleon, who had terrorized much of mainland Europe for a decade

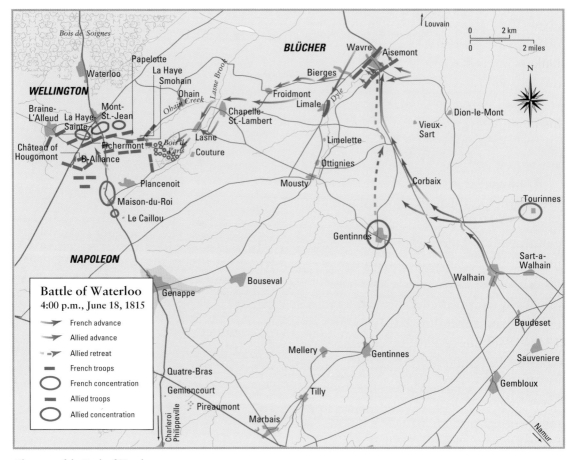

Phase two of the Battle of Waterloo.

and a half, soon capitulated. Napoleon surrendered to Wellington and abdicated as emperor for good.

PRIME MINISTER

Returning to England, Wellington resumed his political career and was a given a position in the Conservative government of Lord Liverpool in 1818. Somewhat

against his wishes, he became prime minister in 1827. He was never to achieve a level of political acclaim to match his military career. In truth, most politicians and the populace would have rather seen him with a sword in his hand than notes for a speech. He became unpopular when he opposed parliamentary reform. Worse, as far as some Protestants were concerned, he failed to oppose Catholic emancipation in 1829. He became known as the Iron Duke—not because of his steadfastness on the plains of war, but because he was forced to put up iron shutters on his London residence (Apsley House, otherwise known as No. 1 London) to stop an angry mob from caving in the windows.

Although he fell from power in 1830, Wellington persisted with his political career. When his party returned to government in 1834, he became prime minister once again—but in less than a month he had given way to Robert Peel. He briefly became foreign secretary under Peel and was a member of the cabinet in 1841–1846, but he failed to convince his party or the public as a politician.

His military exploits, however, were never forgotten, despite the comparative failure of his later career. He was made commander-in-chief of the forces for life in 1842. He died in 1852, but his name lives on in the form of a boot he asked his shoemaker to design, which would be hard-wearing enough for battle but comfortable enough for postwar evening wear. The design of the Wellington boot caught on with the aristocracy for hunting and shooting, and a rubber version became *de rigueur* for farmers everywhere. It is perhaps an odd legacy for one of Britain's most revered military heroes.

FACT FILE

Duke of Wellington

Born: May 1, 1769

Died: September 14, 1852

Birthplace: Dublin, Ireland

Historical Role: First Duke of Wellington

Historic Feats: Earned a knighthood and became a member of parliament as a consequence of his victories in the Mysore War and at Assaye in 1803; removed the French from the entire Iberian Peninsula in 1814; defeated Napoleon for good at the Battle of Waterloo in 1815

Historic Downfalls: Became prime minister in 1827, but was never able to achieve a level of acclaim to match his military career

Hero or Villain: Despite his failings as a politician, Wellington is remembered as one of Britain's greatest military heroes

In truth, most politicians and the populace would have rather seen him with a sword in his hand than notes for a speech.

Simón Bolívar

BORN IN VENEZUELA, WHILE MOST OF SOUTH AMERICA WAS STILL UNDER SPANISH RULE, BOLÍVAR WAS KNOWN AS THE LIBERATOR. HE BROUGHT FREEDOM FROM COLONIAL RULE TO SIX COUNTRIES, INCLUDING BOLIVIA—NAMED IN HIS HONOR.

The son of wealthy Creole parents, (descendents of Spanish settlers), Bolívar was born in 1783 in Caracas. His parents died when he was a child, leaving him a fortune. He was the kind of an aristocratic local man that Spain believed it could rely on to support its vast empire in South America—after all, the nobility existed because of Spanish colonialism. Bolívar had other ideas. He admired both the American and French revolutions that threw off monarchical rule. He finished his education in Europe and was a true child of the Enlightenment; he was influenced by the concepts of rationalism, reason told him that the continued Spanish domination of his homeland was an injustice.

On his return to Venezuela, he joined a group of nationalists that seized control of Caracas in 1810 and expelled the Spanish governor. In the following year, they declared independence from Spain. However, the nationalists lacked the means to keep Venezuela safe from the threat of Spain or France, and so he went to Britain—so often at war with the other two great colonial powers—to seek support. He only secured a promise that Britain would remain neutral, but while there he did manage to convince Francisco de Miranda, a fellow Venezuelan revolutionary, to return to fight for independence.

MIRANDA SURRENDERED TO ENEMY

Back in Venezuela, Bolívar fought under Miranda's command and proved himself a capable leader. However, the Spanish were making inroads in 1812, and Miranda and Bolívar had a series of disagreements that led to Bolívar handing Miranda over to the enemy. The whole country was recaptured by colonial forces and Bolívar had to flee to New Granada (modern-day Colombia), which was also at war with Spain.

Bolivar's campaigns throughout South America.

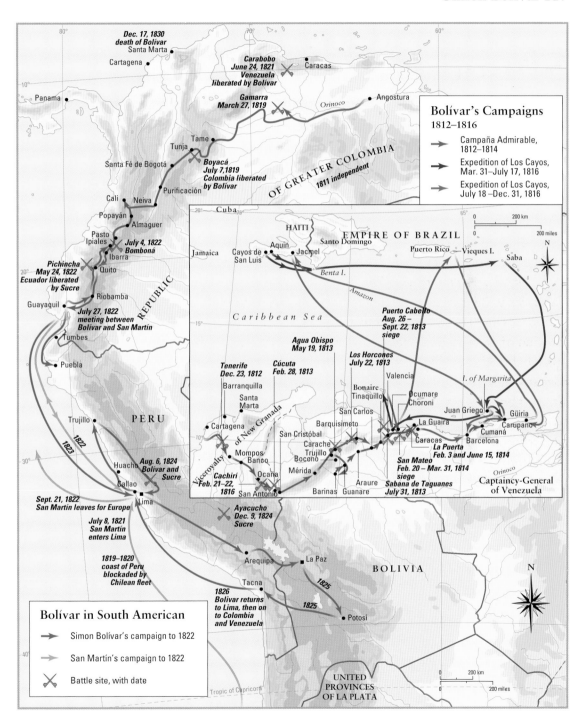

Bolívar's Campaigns
1812–1816

→ Campaña Admirable, 1812–1814

→ Expedition of Los Cayos, Mar. 31–July 17, 1816

→ Expedition of Los Cayos, July 18–Dec. 31, 1816

Bolívar in South American

→ Simon Bolívar's campaign to 1822

→ San Martín's campaign to 1822

✕ Battle site, with date

Dec. 17, 1830 death of Bolívar
Santa Marta
Cartagena

Carabobo June 24, 1821 Venezuela liberated by Bolívar
Caracas

Panama

Gamarra March 27, 1819
Orinoco
Angostura

OF GREATER COLOMBIA
1811 independent

Tame
Tunja
Boyacá July 7,1819 Colombia liberated by Bolívar
Santa Fé de Bogotá
Purificación

Cali
Neiva
Popayán
Almaguer

Pasto
Ipiales
Ibarra
July 4, 1822 Bombona

Pichincha May 24, 1822 Ecuador liberated by Sucre
Quito
Riobamba

Guayaquil
July 27, 1822 meeting between Bolívar and San Martín

REPUBLIC

Tumbes
Puebla

Cuba
HAITI
Santo Domingo
EMPIRE OF BRAZIL
Puerto Rico
Vieques I.
Saba

Jamaica
Cayos de San Luis
Aquin
Jacmel

Benta I.
Amazon

Caribbean Sea

Puerto Cabello Aug. 26 – Sept. 22, 1813 siege

Agua Obispo May 19, 1813

Tenerife Dec. 23, 1812
Cúcuta Feb. 28, 1813
Los Horcones July 22, 1813

Barranquilla
Santa Marta
Valencia
Bonaire
Tinaquillo
Ocumare
Choroni
I. of Margarita

San Carlos
Juan Griego
Güiria

Cartagena
Barquisimeto
La Guaira
Cumaná
Carúpano

of New Granada
San Cristóbal
Carache
Trujillo
Bocono
Caracas
Barcelona

Viceroyalty
Mompos
Banco
Ocaña
Mérida
San Mateo Feb. 20 – Mar. 31, 1814 siege
La Puerta Feb. 3 and June 15, 1814

Cachirí Feb. 21–22, 1816
San Antonio
Barinas
Guanare
Araure
Sabana de Taguanes July 31, 1813
Orinoco

Captaincy-General of Venezuela

PERU

Trujillo

1822
1823

Huacho
Aug. 6, 1824 Bolívar and Sucre
Callao
Lima

Sept. 21, 1822 San Martín leaves for Europe

July 8, 1821 San Martín enters Lima

1819–1820 coast of Peru blockaded by Chilean fleet

Ayacucho Dec. 9, 1824 Sucre

Arequipa
La Paz
BOLIVIA

Tacna
1825
1825
Potosí

1826 Bolívar returns to Lima, then on to Colombia and Venezuela

UNITED PROVINCES OF LA PLATA

Tropic of Capricorn

0   200 km
0   200 miles

0   200 km
0   200 miles

Cuba CORREOS 1983   5

JOSE RAFAEL DE LAS HERAS

BICENTENARIO NACIMIENTO DE SIMON BOLIVAR

Bolivar is still honored in many countries in South America.

He saw the emancipation of the whole region, not just Venezuela, as his just cause. He soon became commander-in-chief of New Granada's revolutionary army and began the "Campaña Admirable" to liberate both territories. He took Caracas in 1813 and Bogotá in 1814. Yet again the lack of supplies, manpower, and an administrative system, as well as local rivalries, let him down and he was forced to flee to the Caribbean. It was there that he took time to reconsider his tactics, mounting a series of naval assaults known as the Expedition of Los Cayos. The Haitian president, Alexandre Pétion, gave him arms and soldiers and he landed in Venezuela in 1816, taking the city of Angostura.

...he broke Spanish colonialism in South America and set the whole northern region on the path to self-determination, and later, to democracy.

LIBERATION

In a daring move, Bolívar then marched on New Granada in 1819, leading 2,500 men through a supposedly impassable route. He took the Spanish by surprise and defeated them at Boyacá, liberating the region. He then organized a congress in Angostura that announced the formation of the republic of Gran Colombia, which combined the modern-day territories of Venezuela, Colombia, Panama, and northern Peru. He became the republic's first president, on December 17, 1819. However, his work was not nearly done and the republic was by no means secure.

He devastated the Spanish forces at Carabobo in Venezuela in 1821, liberating the country, and then marched into Ecuador, emancipating it with the help of Antonio José de Sucre, and adding it to the new republic.

Peru, meanwhile, had its own revolutionary leader, José de San Martin, who had partly liberated the country. Bolívar assumed the task of completing the job and in 1822 became Peru's dictator. He defeated the Spanish cavalry at Junín in 1824 and Sucre decimated the remainder of the Spanish forces at Ayacucho in December, thereby liberating the whole country from Spanish rule. In 1825, Upper Peru became the republic of Bolivia.

Bolívar had become known as "*El Libertador*" during the campaigns. However, among all the praise, it should be remembered that he was an aristocrat who was not really a friend to all classes of people or, indeed, to pure democracy. He wanted a federal state that would be led by the nobility and a benevolent, educated president appointed for life—not by the democratic will of the people. Nonetheless, he broke Spanish colonialism in South America and set the whole northern region on the path to self-determination, and later, to democracy.

GREAT MILITARY CAMPAIGNER

He was president of Gran Colombia in 1821–1830, and oversaw the creation of a league of Hispanic-American states. However, Bolívar was a far greater military campaigner than he was a politician. The new states of his postcolonial utopia soon began warring with each other, and Bolívar lacked the diplomatic skills to ease the rivalries and tensions. He decided to exile himself to Europe, and sadly, at the age of just 47, died during preparations for the voyage to exile.

FACT FILE

Simón Bolívar

Born: July 24, 1783

Died: December 17, 1830

Birthplace: Caracas, Venezuela

Nationality: Venezuelan

Historical Role: Politician and military commander

Marital Alliances: María Teresa Rodríguez del Toro y Alayza (1802)

Historic Feats: Bolívar defeated the Spanish at Boyacá and formed the republic of Gran Colombia, becoming its first president on December 17, 1819. He liberated Colombia, Panama, Venezuela, Ecuador, and Peru from Spanish rule

Hero or Villain: Hero of South American independence

Abraham Lincoln

HE LED THE UNITED STATES THROUGH A DIFFICULT TIME IN ITS HISTORY, WHEN IT WAS SPLIT BY THE ISSUE OF SLAVERY. HIS ACTIONS LED TO ITS ABOLITION, BUT HE WAS ASSASSINATED FIVE DAYS AFTER THE END OF THE CIVIL WAR.

Unlike several of the founding fathers of the United States, Lincoln (the sixteenth president) was not a wealthy, slave-owning member of the landed gentry. He was born in a log cabin in Kentucky in 1809 and became a self-educated lawyer, setting up a practice in Springfield, Illinois, in 1837. He gained a seat in Congress in 1846, but his legal work remained his main concern.

However, one issue close to his heart was to drag him back into the world of politics—slavery. The Missouri Compromise, which had outlawed slavery in the former Louisiana Territory, was repealed in 1854; slavery could now be extended to the new territories of the United States. Lincoln joined the newly formed Republican Party and fought against Senator Stephen Douglas, who had helped to repeal the Compromise in Illinois. "Honest Abe," as he had been known early in his career, lost the election but gained a reputation as an orator. He stood against Douglas again in the 1860 presidential election on a ticket to prevent the extension of slavery.

Lincoln won the election, but before his inauguration seven proslavery states—the Confederacy—proclaimed that they were no longer part of the Union. In his inaugural address in March 1861, he attempted conciliation by saying that he would not legislate against slavery where it was already in existence, but also decreed that no state had the right to secede from the Union. The path to civil war was set. The Confederates demanded that federal troops should leave their garrison at Fort Sumter in Charleston, South Carolina. Lincoln refused the demand, and hostilities soon began.

Lincoln proved to be an excellent wartime leader, directing resources toward the war effort and overseeing the army with aplomb. However, the Confederate

Tactics employed at Gettysburg helped end the Civil War.

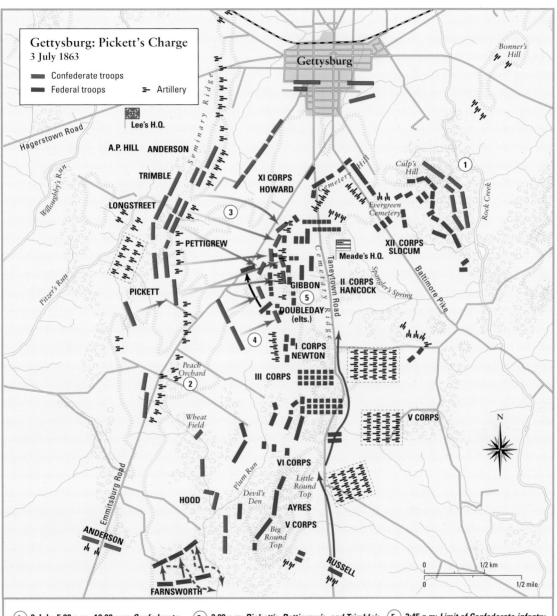

Gettysburg: Pickett's Charge
3 July 1863

- Confederate troops
- Federal troops
- Artillery

Lee's H.Q.

Hagerstown Road

A.P. HILL ANDERSON

Seminary Ridge

TRIMBLE

LONGSTREET

PETTIGREW

PICKETT

Willoughby's Run

Pitzer's Run

XI CORPS
HOWARD

Cemetery Hill

Evergreen Cemetery

Meade's H.Q.

GIBBON

DOUBLEDAY
(elts.)

Cemetery Ridge

Taneytown Road

II CORPS
HANCOCK

Spangler's Spring

XII CORPS
SLOCUM

Culp's Hill

Rock Creek

Baltimore Pike

Bonner's Hill

I CORPS
NEWTON

III CORPS

V CORPS

N

Peach Orchard

Wheat Field

VI CORPS

Plum Run

Devil's Den

Little Round Top

AYRES
V CORPS

Big Round Top

V CORPS

HOOD

Emmitsburg Road

ANDERSON

FARNSWORTH

RUSSELL

0   1/2 km
0   1/2 mile

① **3 July, 5:30 a.m.–10:00 a.m:** *Confederate corps launches repeated attacks on Culp's Hill but makes no progress.*

② **1:00 p.m:** *Confederate artillery cannonade begins with 140 cannons, the Federals reply with 80 guns.*

③ **3:00 p.m:** *Pickett's, Pettigrew's, and Trimble's Confederate infantry attack toward Seminary Ridge.*

④ **3:30 p.m:** *Stannard's Federal brigade attacks flank of Pickett's division.*

⑤ **3:45 p.m:** *Limit of Confederate infantry attacks.*

Abraham Lincoln remains one of America's most beloved presidents.

war was no longer officially just about the secession from the Union, but about the abolition of slavery. At least 20,000 slaves were freed immediately in Union-held sections of those states, while a further three million awaited the advance of the Union armies.

GETTYSBURG

The Confederate army was standing firm and its skillful general, Robert E. Lee, was soon mounting an impressive invasion of the North. It was not until the Battle of Gettysburg in 1863 that the Union forces truly gained the upper hand. Lee's army had reached Pennsylvania where it was met by Major-General John Gordon Meade's army of the Potomac on July 1. The Confederates won the skirmishes on day one of the battle, but on day two both armies had fully assembled and the fighting was far more balanced. Meade laid

forces scored a series of major successes in the early period of the war. Lincoln was bolstered by a major Union riposte at Antietam in September 1862, and issued the "Emancipation Proclamation," decreeing that all slaves in the ten states that were now part of the Confederate rebellion were free (although this was beyond the bounds of the Constitution that the Union had gone to war to protect). This meant that the

He declared...to preserve "a nation conceived in liberty, and dedicated to the proposition that all men are created equal."

out his army in a defensive formation shaped like a hook, bending away at the top to protect his northern flank, and the line held despite significant losses. On the third day, the Confederates repeatedly attacked the end of the hook formation again at Culp's Hill, but the main action focused on "Pickett's Charge"—in which

Major-General George Pickett, under the command of James Longstreet, led a charge of 12,500 men across open ground toward the Union's II Corps under the command of Winfield S. Hancock. Meade had guessed that this would be Lee's tactic after he had failed seriously to damage the Union's flanks, and his artillery and troops were ready. The Confederates were repulsed with heavy losses, effectively putting an end to Lee's assault on Pennsylvania. Following the victory, Lincoln made his famous Gettysburg Address, during which he declared the Union's intention to preserve a "nation conceived in liberty, and dedicated to the proposition that all men are created equal."

ASSASSINATION

The war had turned in favor of the Union, and in 1864 Lincoln was elected for a second term of office, while offering reconciliation to the South with malice toward none, with charity for all. General Lee and his Confederate army surrendered, but John Wilkes Booth, an actor with Confederate sympathies, was not interested in reconciliation. Five days later, on April 15, 1865, he shot and killed Lincoln when the president attended a theater performance. The Thirteenth Amendment to the U.S. Constitution, outlawing slavery throughout the United States, had already been passed by both houses of Congress by the time of Lincoln's assassination and was formally adopted in December 1865. All Americans, whatever their race or color, were finally free before the law.

FACT FILE

Abraham Lincoln

Born: February 12, 1809

Died: April 15, 1865

Birthplace: Kentucky

Historical Role: Sixteenth president of the United States

Marital Alliances: Mary Todd

Historic Feats: Won the presidential election in 1860; issued the Emancipation Proclamation in 1862, immediately freeing 20,000 slaves; his 13th Amendment to the U.S. Constitution outlawed slavery in all the United States. By 1865, all Americans were free before the law

Circumstances of Death: Lincoln was assassinated by John Wilkes Booth on April 15, 1865

Hero or Villain: Hero

Otto von Bismarck

PRINCE VON BISMARCK WAS BORN ON APRIL FOOL'S DAY, 1815, BUT HE WAS NO FOOL. HE UNIFIED GERMANY UNDER HIS CONTROL AND LAUNCHED AN AGGRESSIVE EXPANSIONIST POLICY TO SET UP AN EMPIRE.

O tto von Bismarck bullied his neighboring countries in a manner that many believe set Germany on the path to both world wars of the twentieth century, which would ravage Europe and cost millions of lives. He was a masterful politician and tactical genius who knew no fear. To many, he was also a remorseless egomaniacal villain. Born near Berlin into an aristocratic family, he helped manage his father's estates as a young man. Unlike many of the greatest villains in history, he showed his true colors to the world comparatively late in life, after he became prime minister of Prussia in 1862. Just a week after his appointment by King Wilhelm I, he declared, "The great questions of the time will not be solved by speeches and majority decisions ... but by iron and blood."

PRUSSIAN DOMINANCE

Prussia thought of itself as the powerhouse among the German states (which were separate political entities when Bismarck came to power), but the whole region was subject to the overbearing influence of Austria. The Austrian Empire had emerged out of the Holy Roman Empire at the beginning of the century, encompassing much of central Europe, including modern-day Hungary, Romania, the Balkans, and the Czech Republic, and parts of Germany, Italy, Poland, and the Ukraine. Bismarck

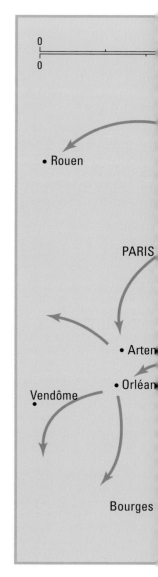

0
0

• Rouen

PARIS

• Arten

• Orléan

Vendôme
•

Bourges

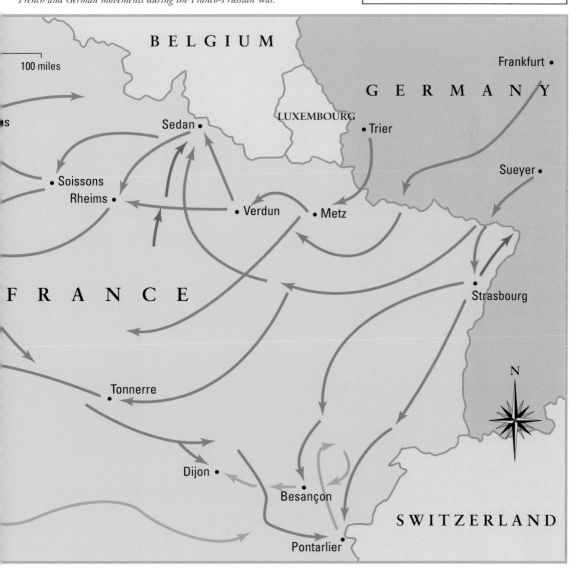

French and German movements during the Franco-Prussian War.

Franco-Prussian War
1870–1871

→ German attacks
→ Imperial French attacks
→ French Republic attacks

used Austria as an ally in his defeat of Denmark in 1865, capturing the provinces of Schleswig and Holstein, but he soon turned on the empire itself. It had been agreed that Holstein should become Austrian territory, but Bismarck overran it with Prussian troops.

In the resulting Seven Weeks' War, the Prussians fought with Austria and its German allies. At the outbreak of the war, Bismarck survived an assassination attempt in which he was shot five times but suffered only minor injuries—the assassin, a democrat who wanted to avert war between the German states, would probably have been successful if he had used a more powerful weapon.

Prussia quickly defeated the Austrian–German forces at the Battle of Königgrätz in July 1866, taking just 8,000 casualties to Austria's 40,000. Prussia took control of several German states, while Austria was forced to agree not to interfere in German affairs. Bismarck was thus able to unify the northern German states into the North German Confederation under his chancellorship.

This was a catastrophic blow to the ambitions and influence of Austria, and Bismarck immediately became one of the most powerful, and threatening, forces in Europe. Not shy of conflict, he then turned his attention to Napoleon III and France. An impressive military and political strategist, he realized that war with France would lead the southern German states into a union with his northern confederation. In the course of the Franco-Prussian War of 1870–1871, he made tremendous inroads into France, getting as far as Rouen and Orléans. He captured Napoleon III, and the new French Republic that emerged in his absence had just as little success against Bismarck's forces. He annexed Alsace-Lorraine from France and, in 1871, he proclaimed the German Empire, which included the southern states. Wilhelm I became the emperor of Germany while Bismarck took the title of prince. He had managed to change the face of Europe in less than a decade.

The Iron Chancellor, as he became known, now needed to secure his gains—and his diplomatic skills emerged. In 1879, he formed an alliance with Austria–Hungary (as the remnant of the Austrian Empire was now known). A couple of years' later, Italy joined the pact, to form the Triple Alliance. This helped Bismarck

> *He annexed Alsace-Lorraine from France and, in 1871, he proclaimed the German Empire, which included the southern states. Wilhelm I became the emperor...*

Otto von Bismarck became known as the Iron Chancellor.

with the new emperor, Wilhelm II, and he was left with little choice but to resign as chancellor on March 18, 1890. He retired to his estates and died on July 30, 1898. He had taken Germany from a group of small, independent states into being the greatest power in mainland Europe.

FACT FILE

Otto von Bismarck

Born: April 1, 1815

Died: July 30, 1898

Birthplace: Schönhausen, Altmark, Prussia

Historical Role: First chancellor of the German Empire

Historic Exploits: Became prime minister in 1862; defeated Denmark in 1865 and the Austrian–German forces at the Battle of Königgrätz in1866; unified the northern German states into the North German Confederation; instigated the Franco-Prussian War and captured Napoleon III; formed the Triple Alliance with Austria-Hungary and Italy

Circumstances of Death: Bismark resigned due to internal friction and retired to his estates, where he died 8 years later

Hero or Villain: Hero of German unification, but a villain to neighboring countries

counteract the continuing threats of France and Russia. He also sought appeasement with Britain in 1887. All this established and preserved the balance of power that would bring peace to Europe until 1914.

Germany may have been secure, but Bismarck's political base was under threat from within. A devout Lutheran Protestant, he despised the influence of the Catholic Church in Germany and sought to undermine it. He also had problems with the growing socialist movement and tried to curtail it by introducing pensions and antisocialist legislation. However, internal frictions led to disagreements

Florence Nightingale

NURSING WAS REGARDED AS UNSUITABLE
WORK FOR UPPER- OR MIDDLE-CLASS
WOMEN IN THE NINETEENTH CENTURY,
BUT FLORENCE NIGHTINGALE ALMOST
SINGLE-HANDEDLY CHANGED THIS.

Florence Nightingale raised the profile of the "caring profession" through her work in the Crimean War and at home in Britain. However, while introducing new standards of care and trying to save lives, her lack of sanitary techniques led to the deaths of many soldiers. She rapidly learnt from her mistakes and pushed forward the boundaries of hospital care effectively. Those who learnt from her work would save the lives of millions across the world.

Florence Nightingale was born in 1820 to a well-to-do British family in Florence (thus her name). When she grew up, she wanted to be a nurse, but women of her

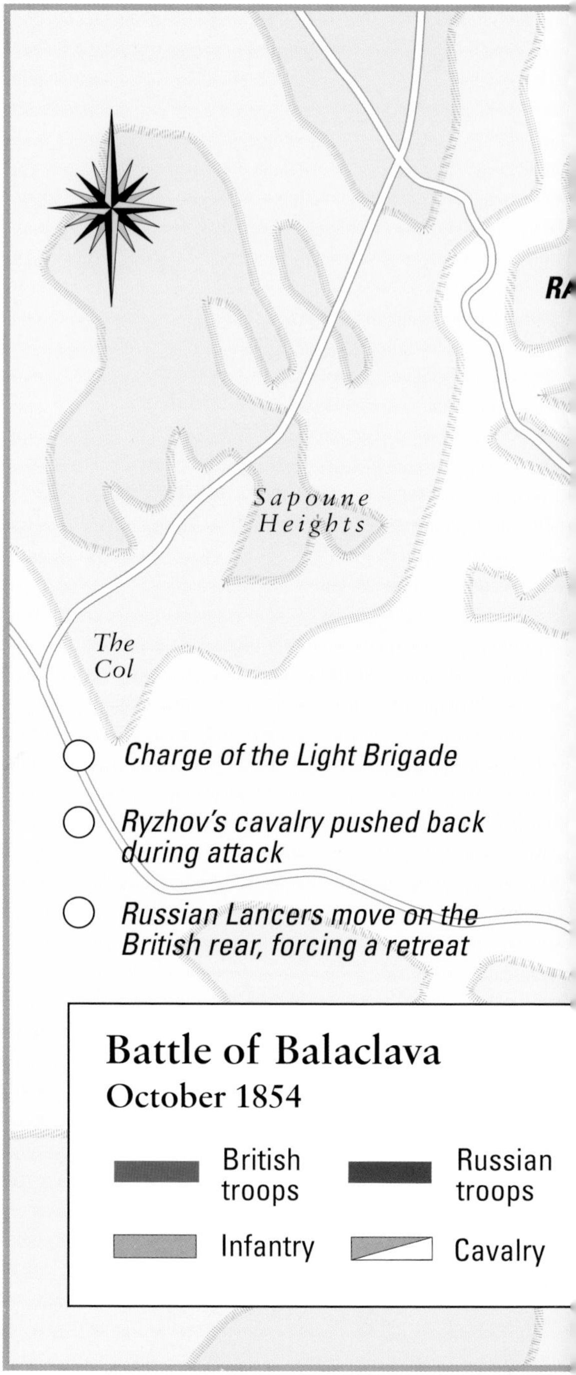

The battle of Balaclava resulted in huge loss of life.

RA

Sapoune Heights

The Col

◯ **Charge of the Light Brigade**

◯ **Ryzhov's cavalry pushed back during attack**

◯ **Russian Lancers move on the British rear, forcing a retreat**

Battle of Balaclava
October 1854

	British troops		Russian troops
	Infantry		Cavalry

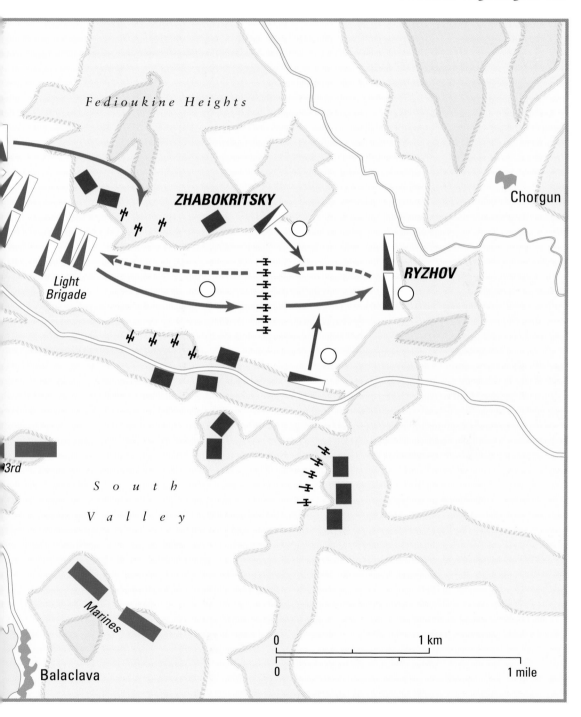

Fedioukine Heights

ZHABOKRITSKY

Chorgun

RYZHOV

*Light
Brigade*

S o u t h

V a l l e y

3rd

Marines

Balaclava

0		1 km
0		1 mile

Florence Nightingale's influence revolutionized nursing.

class did not work; Her parents thought the work was beneath her and expected her to make a good marriage and settle down. Nightingale was determined to pursue her ambition and her parents eventually relented in 1851. In the absence of proper nursing training in Britain at that time, she went to Germany to study. She returned to Britain to become superintendent at a hospital for "Sick Gentlewomen" in London's Harley Street in 1853.

ABSENCE OF MEDICAL FACILITIES

The Crimean War, in which the French and British allied against Russia in a bid to control the failing Ottoman Empire, started in the following year. Britain incurred heavy losses and the newspapers carried reports of the absence of any proper medical facilities to treat wounded British soldiers. The war minister Sidney Herbert was aware of Nightingale's devotion to nursing and asked her to take a team of nurses to the military hospitals in Turkey. They left on October 21, 1854.

The need for the nurses became even more apparent just four days later, when the British suffered one of the most famous disasters in their entire military history. The Battle of Balaclava on October 25 was induced when the French and British prepared to capture the Russian port of Sebastopol. British and Ottoman troops under the command of Lord Raglan moved toward the port of Balaclava, but the force of just 4,500 men was met by a huge army of 25,000 Russians.

The Russian cavalry, under the command of Lieutenant-General Ryzhov, charged at the severely outnumbered Scottish 93rd Highland Regiment, which formed what became known as the "Thin Red Line" due to their red jackets and lack of numbers. The line held, and the Heavy Brigade was then able to push back the cavalry, forcing the Russians into a defensive position. However, at that point, the Light Brigade misunderstood an order from Raglan and bravely charged headlong at the main body of the Russian army with just 666 men. They fought heroically but 110 were slain and over 160 were wounded in just 20 minutes.

FILTHY CONDITIONS

Nightingale and her team of 38 volunteer nurses finally arrived at the British barracks in Scutari, now known as Üsküdar in Istanbul, a month after the fateful Charge of the Light Brigade. She encountered severe problems—there was hardly any medicine, the conditions were filthy, and the staff were overworked and improperly trained. Infection was rife. Early in the twentieth century, it was claimed that her actions reduced the death rate in the Crimean War hospital from about 50 percent to just 2 percent, but this was not a claim she made herself. The death rate actually rose after her arrival. At this point in her career, she was not really aware of the benefits of sanitation. In her first winter more than 4,000 soldiers died in the hospital, the vast majority of them from cholera, dysentery, typhus, and other diseases caused by the insanitary conditions, not from the wounds they had suffered on the battlefield. In time, better sewage maintenance and ventilation improved conditions at Scutari, and the nurses were able to apply their newfound professionalism more effectively. Nightingale learned from the situation, and would later help to initiate the sanitary design of hospitals and the importance to health of good living conditions. Her work made her famous throughout Britain and beyond as "The Lady with the Lamp," a name derived from a *Times* report describing her making her rounds in a military hospital. More importantly, her experiences and work highlighting the benefits of proper trained nursing was brought to the attention of governments, hospital benefactors, and the military.

...it was claimed that her actions reduced the death rate in the Crimean War hospital from about 50 percent to just 2 percent, but this was not a claim she herself made.

On her return from the Crimea, Nightingale wrote the classic text, *Notes on Nursing*. In 1860, she founded the Nightingale School and Home for Nurses in London, having raised huge donations to fund her work. In 1907, she received the Order of Merit, three years before her death at the grand old age of 90 (the average life expectancy at that time was only 50 years).

Ned Kelly

By 1880, THE YOUNG AUSTRALIAN BUSHRANGER NED KELLY HAD BECOME THE MOST NOTORIOUS OUTLAW IN THE WORLD, HAVING GUNNED DOWN SEVERAL POLICE OFFICERS AND GONE ON A SPREE OF ROBBERIES.

Edward "Ned" Kelly was born in Beveridge, Victoria, Australia, in June 1855, the son of an Irish convict. He was dead by the age of 25, but his legend endures. He is remembered as an enigmatic folk hero and callous villain in equal measure. The romantic idea of Ned Kelly and his headline-grabbing feats depicts him as a brave gunman standing up to the corrupt colonial authorities who persecuted his family. In any case, it did not take long for Ned to follow in his father's footsteps and spend the rest of his life on the wrong side of the law.

EARLY CRIMES

As a teenager, Ned was a minor criminal who faced various charges involving assault and robbery. Some of these charges may well have been trumped up by the police, who had decided that the Kelly clan were nothing but troublemakers. Ned served three years' hard labor for being in possession of a stolen horse, which he apparently thought was the rightful property of an associate, and in his absence his family continued to face seemingly erroneous charges for horse theft. The Kellys felt victimized, but on his release the 19-year-old Ned and his younger brother Daniel were undoubtedly involved in horse rustling.

RISE TO FAME

Ned's national notoriety arose in April 1878, when Constable Alexander Fitzpatrick attempted to arrest Daniel and, according to one version of events, tried to assault their sister Kate. When the family intervened and sent Fitzpatrick packing, the constable claimed that Dan, Ned (who had not even been present), their mother, and associates had attempted to murder him. Fitzpatrick's evidence was accepted, although he was later dismissed from the police for perjury and drunkenness. The Kellys' mother was arrested and imprisoned, while the boys went on the run.

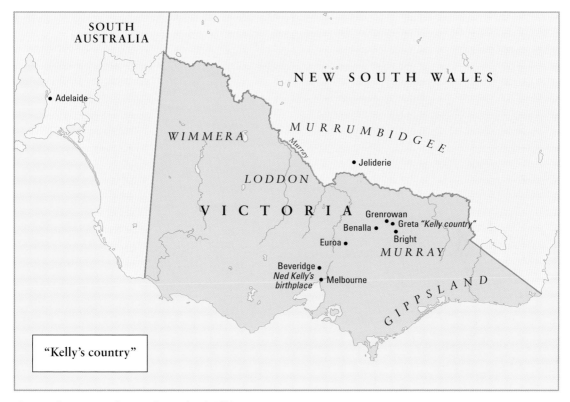

The state of Victoria was the scene of most of Ned Kelly's activity.

The Victoria police were even more determined to eradicate the troublesome Kellys. Knowing this pushed the brothers up to a new level of recklessness—along with two associates they raided the camp of a police search party and killed three officers. They were now officially outlaws, with a reward of £500 on their heads.

Perhaps thinking that they had nothing to lose, the Kelly Gang conducted two major robberies, on banks in Euroa in 1878 and Jeliderie in 1879. However,

Ned and his men still held their lives to be precious. They had metal plow blades beaten into shape to act as suits of armour that would protect them from the bullets of the police. The suits also included cylindrical helmets with slits for their eyes.

THE FINAL BATTLE

After a two-year adventure in which their fame grew, and the newspapers even printed Ned's defense of his actions and his claims of police persecution, the

Ned Kelly's homemade armor, located at the State Library of Victoria, Melbourne, Australia.

Kellys' escapades finally came to an end. On June 1880, the brothers killed police informer Aaron Sherritt, and started another gunfight with the police before escaping. Afterward, the Kelly Gang knew that the police would follow them to Glenrowan using a special police train to move the officers as quickly as possible. The Kellys prepared to ambush the train by cutting telegraph wires and ripping up the railroad tracks, and they took several dozen hostages at the local hotel.

However, the police were forewarned and stopped the train before it could be derailed. They then laid siege to the hotel in a nine-and-a-half hour battle. Severely outnumbered, Ned Kelly, dressed in his helmet and suit of armor, escaped from the hotel and single-handedly attacked the police from the rear, blazing away with his gun. He was shot around 20 times and wounded in the hand, arm, leg, and groin, but the armor protected his head and torso and he survived. He was captured, but Daniel's charred remains were found after the police had burnt the hotel down to the ground. Ned was hanged in Old Melbourne Gaol on November 11, 1880. When informed that the hour of his execution had been set, he merely said, "Such is life."

NED'S LEGACY

Many Australians continue to regard Kelly as a national hero who bravely fought the corrupt authorities in their homeland, while others believe him to have been a cold-hearted cop killer. However, in heritage terms, Australia's long-held admiration for antiauthoritarianism has won the day. The location of Ned Kelly's last stand is now a national heritage site, while Sidney Nolan's painting *First Class Marksman*, depicting Ned Kelly in his peculiar armor, became the most expensive

Ned Kelly has become a folk hero in Australia.

FACT FILE

Ned Kelly

Born: June 1855

Died: November 11, 1880

Birthplace: Beveridge, Victoria, Australia

Historical Role: Australian bushranger and outlaw

Historic Feats: The Kelly Gang raided the camp of a police search party, killing three officers, and conducted two major raids on banks in Euroa (1878) and Jeliderie (1879)

Circumstances of Death: Ned was hanged in Old Melbourne Gaol after the police finally captured him

Hero or Villain: Many Australians consider Ned a national hero, while others think him a villainous criminal

work by an Australian artist when it sold for AUS$5.4 million in 2010. Numerous movies and books are dedicated to the exploits of the outlaw.

Kelly's body was dumped in a mass grave in Melbourne. Its whereabouts remained a mystery, but it was thought that his bones were moved to another mass grave at Pentridge Prison in 1929. In 2009, the remains of 34 bodies at Pentridge were exhumed and following DNA tests, a headless skeleton was identified as that of Ned Kelly.

The Victoria police were now even more determined to eradicate the troublesome Kellys. Knowing this seemed to push the brothers up to a new level of recklessness

Cecil Rhodes

THERE ARE NOT MANY PEOPLE WHO
HAVE A LARGE COUNTRY NAMED AFTER
THEM, BUT CECIL RHODES WAS ONE.
HOWEVER, HIS LEGACY CRUMBLED
ALONG WITH THE BRITISH EMPIRE.

Rhodes was born in Hampshire, UK, in 1853, the son of a vicar. A sickly boy, he was sent to South Africa when he was 17 to improve his health. Instead, he saw it as an opportunity to seek his fortune—and there he found it, many times over, becoming one of the richest men the world had ever known. He left Natal to go to the diamond fields of Kimberley and started buying up small mines in the area.

He was no friend to black African rights, though, especially as he relied on cheap labor, working in appalling conditions, to maintain his wealth.

He returned to Britain to study at Oxford University, while maintaining his mining interests, and soon began to buy more expensive claims, including that of the De Beers family. Along with associate Charles Rudd, Rhodes set up the De Beers Consolidated Mines and Goldfields of South Africa Ltd. in 1880, with Rhodes at its head. He rapidly amassed a fortune from diamonds and, later, fruit farming, but he shared that particular English penchant for setting up political and administrative systems in a foreign land that he was simultaneously bleeding dry of its natural resources.

He joined the Cape legislature in 1881 and set upon a political career spurred on by a desire to create a South African federation of territories under the control of the British Empire. He wanted to establish British-controlled land all the way from the Cape to Cairo to allow its natural resources to be tapped exclusively by his countrymen.

As part of this grand ambition, he annexed Bechuanaland (modern-day Botswana) in 1885, and then formed the British South Africa Company in 1889. Like the East India Company, this was a quasigovernmental, quasimilitary, quasicommercial entity, which he used to occupy Mashonaland and Matabeleland. In 1895, they were formally renamed, without too much modesty, as Rhodesia. Rhodes' love of Britain and its empire was fulsome—in his first will, he expressed his desire to create a "Secret Society, the true aim and object whereof shall be for the extension of British rule throughout the world." However, he wanted colonial British interests in southern Africa to run the territory,not distant bureaucrats in Britain.

Rhodes became prime minister of the British Cape Colony in 1890, and believed that the Boer Republic of the Transvaal also should be run by British interests. In the last days of 1896, the British statesman Leander Starr Jameson and policemen from Bechuanaland and Rhodesia raided the Transvaal in an attempt to trigger an uprising by British workers in the region. The attempted coup was a disaster and the uprising failed to materialize. Rhodes' brother Frank was implicated and he was charged with high treason for his part in the affair; Cecil was also implicated and had to resign. The incident opened the door to the Second Boer War and the British dominance over the region became fragile. The Boer and the British states finally united as the Union of South Africa in 1910.

LEGACY OF THE EMPIRE

Despite the Jameson Raid, Rhodes was something of a friend to the Afrikaans in the Cape Colony, and he continued to put forward the dictum "Equal rights for every civilized man south of the Zambezi." He was no friend to black African rights, though, especially as he relied on cheap labor, who were compelled to work in appalling conditions, to maintain his wealth. Rhodes was initially a hero in Britain, as more than any other individual he typified the kind of adventurous imperial character that had allowed the small island to punch above its weight, supposedly bringing civilization and administrative sophistication to the peoples of foreign lands. Like every large empire in history, the British Empire was too big to sustain itself, and the indigenous races would eventually find the strength to push away the colonial rulers in order to pursue their own path. As soon as they were able to declare independence, Northern Rhodesia and Southern Rhodesia became Zambia and Zimbabwe.

Rhodes' De Beers company still trades in almost half the world's rough diamonds, and Rhodes is a notable figure in the political history of South Africa. However, in Britain the idea that this rich colonialist and subjugator of foreign peoples could be a hero is now too muddied a concept to support, so there are few monuments to his greatness (unlike in South Africa). Perhaps his enduring legacy in the UK is the Rhodes scholarship system funded by his estate, which support students from the U.S., the Commonwealth, and Germany in their studies at Oxford University. Beneficiaries have included many leading figures, such as ex-president Bill Clinton and musician Kris Kristofferson.

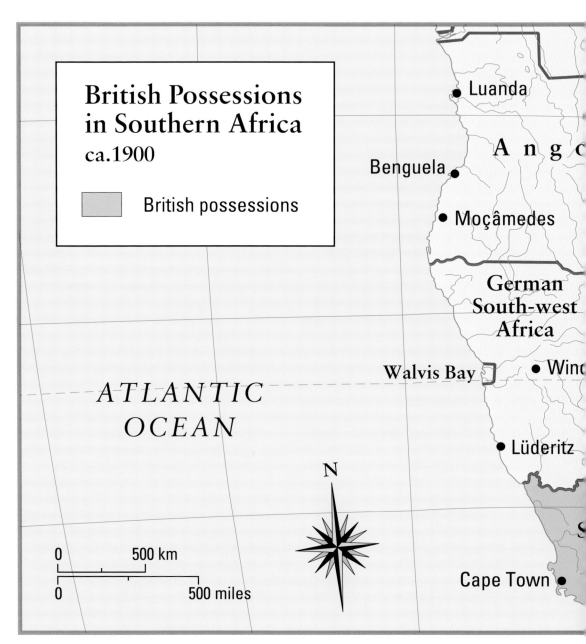

British Possessions
in Southern Africa
ca.1900

British possessions

Luanda

A n g o

Benguela

Moçâmedes

German
South-west
Africa

Walvis Bay

Win

ATLANTIC
OCEAN

Lüderitz

N

0   500 km

0   500 miles

Cape Town

S

The political map of southern Africa at the turn of the nineteenth century.

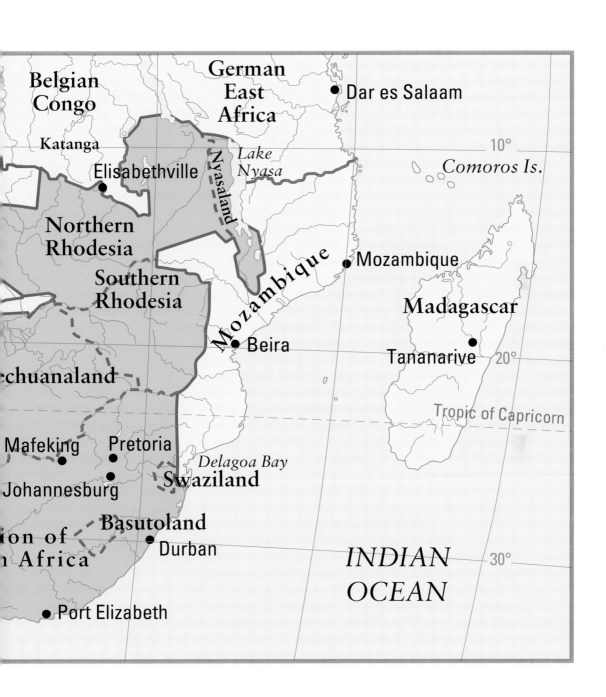

Belgian
Congo

German
East
Africa

Dar es Salaam

Katanga

10°

Elisabethville

Lake
Nyasa

Comoros Is.

Nyasaland

Northern
Rhodesia

Southern
Rhodesia

Mozambique

Mozambique

Madagascar

Beira

Tananarive

20°

chuanaland

0

Tropic of Capricorn

Mafeking

Pretoria

Delagoa Bay

Johannesburg

Swaziland

Basutoland

INDIAN

ion of
1 Africa

Durban

30°

OCEAN

Port Elizabeth

TWENTIETH CENTURY

This century was packed with conflict—
wars, revolutions, and struggles—all
giving rise to global figures. Emmeline
Pankhurst, Mahatma Gandhi, Martin
Luther King Jr., and Mother Teresa can all
be classified as heroes. More ambivalent
are the legacies of great South American
revolutionary Che Guevara and China's
"Great Leader" Mao—both are revered by
many millions around the globe, but have
also attracted huge criticism. Likewise,
the mostly positive reputations of Winston
Churchill and President John F. Kennedy
are occasionally questioned by a more
objective look back at their records. Even
Oskar Schindler, the man who rescued
many Jewish people from certain death,
has his critics. But there are some definite
villains—mad Russian monk Rasputin,
Josef Stalin, Mussolini, Hitler, Pol Pot, and
Idi Amin have all been classified
as villainous monsters.

Emmeline Pankhurst

AT THE CLOSE OF THE NINETEENTH CENTURY, WOMEN STILL DID NOT HAVE THE RIGHT TO VOTE IN THE UNITED STATES OR IN BRITAIN. A RADICAL MIDDLE-CLASS WOMAN WOULD MAKE SURE THAT WOMEN FINALLY ACHIEVED THIS RIGHT.

Emmeline Goulden was born in Manchester, England, in 1858 into a progressive family that encouraged its children to have radical views on the world. At the age of 21, she married Richard Pankhurst, a lawyer who believed in women's suffrage—the right to vote— and was involved in changing the property laws in favor of women. Emmeline and her husband founded the Women's Franchise League, which campaigned to allow married women to vote in local elections. After Richard's death in 1898, her outspoken radicalism really began to emerge on a national scale. An excellent speaker, able to draw people toward her cause, she cofounded the women-only Women's Social and Political Union (WSPU) in 1903. It became a militant organization and its members, who campaigned for the right of women to vote in all political elections, were christened "suffragettes." At home, Emmeline initially had the ardent support of her daughters,

Christabel, Sylvia, and Adela; Christabel eventually became the political leader of the movement.

The violence of the campaign, and the extent to which women—including privileged, upper-class women—would put their own safety in danger, shocked society. According to convention, they were supposed to be at home looking after their families or pursuing trivial pursuits deemed suitable for a woman of standing, such as sewing or learning a new song on the piano. Instead, from 1905 they were marching on the street, carrying banners, shouting, and singing slogans, and defying the police. Their campaign took on an even more aggressive edge as the suffragettes began breaking windows and setting fire to buildings. Many of the women were jailed for their offenses. Britain had never seen anything like it. The suffragettes' resoluteness shook society to its core. In a speech on February 16, 1912, Pankhurst said, "Is not a woman's

Emmeline Pankhurst (right) with her daughter Christabel.

Pankhurst was imprisoned for her suffragette protests.

life, is not her health, are not her limbs more valuable than panes of glass? There is no doubt of that, but most important of all, does not the breaking of glass produce more effect upon the government?"

HUNGER STRIKES AND FORCE-FEEDING

And yet there was more to come. The imprisoned suffragettes began a series of hunger strikes, but the authorities responded by force-feeding them, pushing tubes down their throats, often with violence, and consequently making the women ill. Leading the protests, Emmeline Pankhurst was arrested several times and was subjected to violent force-feeding while on hunger-strike. Society at the time was appalled at this treatment of women, which was brought to light by the likes of Lady Constance Lytton, who wrote about her experiences in prison and revealed that working-class suffragettes were more likely to be force-fed than upper-class women. As a result of public anxiety, the government quickly had to introduce an act, nicknamed the 'Cat and Mouse Act', by which women would be released if they became ill but rearrested if their condition improved. Sylvia Pankhurst was imprisoned nine times under the act.

Perhaps the most shocking action of the suffragette movement occurred on June 4, 1913, when Emily Davison, a WSPU member, took drastic action due to the government's continued refusal to grant the vote to women. During the Epsom Derby, a showpiece event in the horse-racing calendar, Davison walked out onto the track and stepped in front of a galloping horse owned by King George V. She died of her injuries four days later. By this time, not all WSPU members were happy about the organization's activities and political stance. Several leading members left, including Sylvia Pankhurst, causing a rift in the family.

WAR INTERVENES

The militant action suddenly came to an end in 1914 at the outbreak of World War I. Emmeline Pankhurst then diverted her considerable energies to the war effort. However, her work in aid of women's suffrage had already completely shifted the political climate in favor of votes for women. In 1918, almost as soon as World War I had ended, the Representation of the People Act gave the right to vote to women at the age of 30 and over.

One might expect Emmeline Pankhurst to have had liberal or even socialist views in all matters, but her politics shifted to the right in later years. She feared communism and became a supporter of the right-wing Conservative party, the most traditional of the parties whose policies usually attempted to maintain the status quo. She even campaigned as

a prospective parliamentary candidate for the Conservatives in 1926. She died on June 14, 1928, shortly after the voting age for women was reduced to 21 to match that of men. Women's suffrage is surely her true legacy, for which she is still considered a great feminist heroine.

FACT FILE

Emmeline Pankhurst

Born: July 14, 1858

Died: June 14, 1928

Birthplace: Manchester, England

Historical Role: Political campaigner and leader of the suffragette movement

Marital Alliances: Richard Pankhurst (1879)

Historic Feats: Cofounded the Women's Franchise League and the WSPU (1903); led an active political campaign for women's suffrage from 1905

Legacy: Pankhurst's work shifted the political climate in favor of women's suffrage. In 1918, the Representation of the People Act gave the vote to women at the age of 30 and over. In 1928, the voting age for women was reduced to 21

Hero or Villain: Suffragette heroine

Rasputin

DESPITE HIS NAME BEING SYNONYMOUS WITH EVIL AND DEBAUCHERY (RASPUTIN MEANS 'DEBAUCHED ONE'), RASPUTIN HELD SWAY OVER THE WIFE OF RUSSIAN CZAR NICHOLAS II, ONE OF THE MOST POWERFUL WOMEN IN THE WORLD.

Rasputin's real name was Grigori Yefimovich Novyk, who was born in 1869 to Siberian peasants. He became an Eastern Orthodox mystic who wandered around the country. A strangely beguiling figure with a strong personality and eyes that could supposedly transfix people, including his multiple sexual conquests, he gained a reputation for being able to cure the sick with supernatural powers. In 1905, he even convinced the czarina (she was the granddaughter of Queen Victoria) that he could help her son Alexei's condition of hemophilia, stopping his bleeding possibly through the use of hypnotism. She consequently had great faith in this strange man, who became a favorite at the royal court in St. Petersburg. He took to advising the czar and czarina as if his opinion was ordained by God, and Nicholas gave some

He convinced the czarina that he could help her son Alexei's condition of hemophilia ... she had great faith in this strange man, who became a favorite ...

value to his views because he believed Rasputin represented the thoughts of the peasantry, with whom the czar otherwise had almost no contact.

With long hair in a center parting and a straggly beard, he was shockingly debauched, setting up wild parties in which people would follow his maxim of sinning in order to gain forgiveness. He is even thought to have slept with the czarina herself—a telegram from her to Rasputin reads, "I sacrifice my husband and my heart to you. Pray and bless. Love and kisses—darling." However, Prime Minister Pyotr Stolypin was not taken in by Rasputin, who had once tried to hypnotize him. He ordered an investigation into Rasputin's scandalous activities and had him removed from St. Petersburg. The czarina detested Stolypin as a result and, when he was assassinated

Rasputin made an odd figure at the Russian court.

Rasputin at the heart of a glamorous gathering.

in 1911, she brought Rasputin back to court. It was not just his outrageous behavior that insulted Russian nobles. When Nicholas left Alexandra in charge of the country's internal matters so that he could take personal charge of the war with Germany in 1915, Rasputin began to have great influence over ecclesiastical and political appointments. He claimed he was given insight by God himself, but many of the appointments brought clearly incompetent people into positions of power. He was also thought to have accepted bribes and sexual favors in exchange for royal influence, and he had become a drunkard, although some of the rumors about him were concocted by the Bolshevik Communists.

Meanwhile, Nicholas was completely mismanaging the conflict with Germany during World War I, having already lost almost the entire Russian fleet in the earlier Russo–Japanese War. The population was increasingly appalled by the great loss of life incurred under his erratic leadership, thereby helping the Bolsheviks gain popularity across the country. Some believed that the czarina (German by descent) and Rasputin were German agents, wielding a destructive influence over Nicholas. The nobles believed that the notoriety of this peculiar upstart was harming the reputation of the monarchy, and they took the decision to kill him in December 1916. According to somewhat dubious accounts, this proved harder than they thought.

First of all, they tried to poison him with wine and cakes laced with cyanide. Despite consuming enough poison to kill five men, it had no effect. Consequently, the main assassin, Prince Yusupov, shot him at point-blank range. Later, when the prince lent over the supposedly dead body, Rasputin opened his eyes and grabbed him in a strong grip. One historian claims that Yusupov may have botched the shooting on purpose because he was secretly in love with the mad monk. His colleagues, who may have included members of the British secret service, then shot Rasputin three more times, but he was still alive, so they started clubbing him to death. Even this didn't work. They bound his body and dumped it in the icy Neva river. This turned out to be a wise move, because the autopsy report revealed that he had died from drowning.

MONARCHY DAMAGED

Rasputin's presence in the court irreparably damaged the reputation of the already inept czar, who appeared to be taking advice from a morally corrupt and conniving madman. The czar and czarina would only survive for a short while after Rasputin's death. The revolutions of 1917 swept the Romanovs from power, and in the following year they were murdered. In the meantime, Bolshevik soldiers dug up Rasputin's body from its burial ground in the czar's palace and burned it in an effort to make sure that the evil madman never rose from the dead again.

FACT FILE

Rasputin

Born: January 22, 1869

Died: December 26, 1916

Birthplace: Pokrovskoye, Russia

Historical Role: Eastern Orthodox mystic and advisor to Czar Nicholas II and Czarina Alexandra of Russia

Religion: Russian Orthodox

Circumstances of Death: Prince Yusupov and his band of conspirators murdered Rasputin

Legacy: The czar and czarina's reputations were severely damaged by their closeness to Rasputin

Hero or Villain: Rasputin is often seen as a corrupt and self-serving villain, but he was also a victim of prejudice and murder

Mahatma Gandhi

AN INDIAN NATIONALIST WHO HELPED HIS COUNTRY THROW OFF THE CHAINS OF BRITISH COLONIALISM WHILE ADVOCATING PEACEFUL MEANS, GANDHI REMAINS A WORLDWIDE SYMBOL OF PACIFISM AND PEACEFUL RESISTANCE.

Mohandas Karamchand Gandhi was born on October 2, 1869 in Porbandar, while India was under British rule. He studied law in London and practiced as a lawyer, settling in South Africa. It was there that his political activism and lifelong pursuit of a fair, nondiscriminatory society emerged, as he led the Indian community in its fight against racial prejudice. His was imprisoned many times, but the government eventually agreed to some of his demands.

He returned to India in 1915 and gained millions of followers in his campaigns against excessive taxes and discrimination. He became the leader of the Indian National Congress in 1921, advocating a policy of nonviolent noncooperation with the British authorities. The policy, which he had originated in South Africa, was known as *satyagraha* (which roughly translates as "devotion to truth"). He was imprisoned for two years from 1922 on charges of sedition. He wanted to lead the nation out of colonialism but without war or any violent action, because this was against his principles. Instead, he organized hunger strikes, episodes of civil disobedience, and a boycott of British goods. In 1930, he led a 250 mile (400 km) "salt march" and the mass breaking of the British salt laws, which had allowed Britain to monopolize the production of salt. It laid down the marker that the huge populace of India would no longer kowtow to the self-interested policies of Britain. The British administration was worried enough to invite Gandhi to a conference in London in the following year, where they discussed the possibility of Indian independence but without any firm resolution. He left the Indian National Congress in 1934 in protest against the use of violence.

DEVOUT AND TOLERANT

Gandhi also campaigned for social reform and advocated religious tolerance. He was a

The political map of the Indian sub-continent at Independence and Partition.

Gandhi remains a symbol of peaceful resistance.

devout Hindu (but also learnt from aspects of other religions, including Jainism), and became known as Mahatma, which is Sanskrit for "Great Soul." He was a strict vegetarian and only wore a *dhoti*, a single piece of white cloth wrapped around his body. From the mid-1930s, he led a life of simplicity in a remote village without electricity or running water. Hinduism was the majority religion in India, but there were a great many Muslims in the country, as well as Christians, Sikhs, Buddhists, and Jainists, and Gandhi was adamant

that the followers of the different creeds could live together without conflict. He also called for an end to discrimination by caste, particularly against the Dalits (the "Untouchables"), whose prospects were limited solely because of their lowly caste.

INDEPENDENCE AND PARTITION

Gandhi escalated his demands for independence in 1942, asking every Indian to lay down their life, if it became necessary, in the cause of freedom. In the face of mass opposition, Britain, considerably weakened as a colonial force over the course of the first half of the twentieth century, had little choice but to grant India independence in 1947. Gandhi was regarded as the official "Father of the Nation." However, independence came at a great cost both to Gandhi's ideals of religious harmony and to him personally.

Britain took into account Muslim demands for a separate Muslim state and India was partitioned, with the Muslim states of West Pakistan and East Pakistan (the latter became Bangladesh) created in the north. The partition caused chaos, and violence erupted, just as Gandhi feared that it would. He had once said, "An eye for an eye only ends up making the whole world blind." About 14 million people were displaced, with 7 million Hindus and Sikhs leaving their homes within the new

Pakistani states, while the same number of Muslims headed the other way. There were devastating riots and confrontations and many people lost their lives in the ensuing violence. The British partition also failed to deal with the disputed region of Kashmir, which exploded into war and remains a focal point of conflict between India and Pakistan to this day.

ASSASSINATED BY AN EXTREMIST

Gandhi did not take part in the celebrations of Independence, and instead concentrated on trying to stop the violence. Several hundred thousand people died as a result of the partition, with the most famous victim being Gandhi himself. He was assassinated on January 30, 1948, by Nathuram Godse, a Hindu extremist who hated Gandhi's attempts to appease Muslims. He was shot three times on his way into a prayer meeting.

The Indian Constitution embraced many of Gandhi's principles, including outlawing discrimination by caste, although the caste system itself still exists. His mantra of nonviolent noncooperation in the face of injustice is still praised. The day of his death is observed annually as Martyrs' Day in India. His method of nonviolent protest has influenced civil rights movements around the world and he remains a role model for peaceful change.

FACT FILE

Mahatma Gandhi

Born: October 2, 1869

Died: January 30, 1948

Birthplace: Porbandar, India

Historical Role: Political activist and leader of Indian nationalism

Historic Feats: Gandhi became the leader of the Indian National Congress in 1921. India was granted independence from Britain in 1947, and Gandhi became the "Father of the Nation"

Circumstances of Death: Gandhi was assassinated on January 30, 1948 by Hindu extremist Nathuram Godse

Legacy: The Indian Constitution embraced many of Gandhi's principles. The day of his death is annually observed as Martyrs' Day in India

Hero or Villain: Hero of Indian independence and of nonviolent protest

Gandhi escalated his demands for independence in 1942, asking every Indian to lay down their life, if it became necessary, in the cause of freedom.

Joseph Stalin

FROM COMMUNIST HERO TO RUTHLESS DESPOT, STALIN'S REPUTATION HAS UNDERGONE A SEISMIC SHIFT SINCE HIS DEATH. HE TURNED THE SOVIET UNION INTO A SUPERPOWER, BUT AT THE COST OF MILLIONS OF INNOCENT LIVES.

Joseph Vissarionovich Dzhugashvili adopted the name Stalin, which means "steel"—reflecting his determination to show no compassion to his own people and enemies alike. The son of a shoemaker, he was born in 1869 in Georgia (then part of the Russian Empire) and educated for the priesthood. He was expelled from the seminary (for distributing Marxist propaganda, according to Soviet mythology, but actually for missing some exams). In 1903, he joined Lenin's Bolshevik Communist party, which opposed the ruling czardom of the Russia Empire. He was repeatedly arrested and expelled to Siberia for his part in Bolshevik activities.

After the Communists took power in 1917, he became a member of Lenin's cabinet and attracted his own followers. He was general secretary of the Communist party from 1922, and became head of the government after the death of Lenin in 1924. He wanted to create "socialism in one country," but faced an ideological battle with Leon Trotsky. In 1927, Stalin managed to have Trotsky expelled from the Communist party and then exiled from the country. Stalin effectively became the dictator of the Soviet Union (as the former Russian Empire had been rechristened). His dislike of his old foe never ceased and he had Trotsky assassinated in Mexico in 1940, despite the fact that he was no longer any real threat to the regime.

FIVE-YEAR PLANS

From 1928, Stalin began to collectivize under state control all industry and agriculture in the Soviet Union. He created a system of five-year plans, setting productivity targets that were difficult or impossible to attain. Industry was able to progress quite rapidly, but centralization initially destroyed agricultural productivity. The farmers (*kulaks*) were forcibly dispossessed, and the disruption to farming

Russia and its sphere of influence during Stalin's reign.

Stalin's Europe

- Soviet Bloc
- Soviet sympathy
- NATO member (1949–1959)
- Nonaligned or neutral
- Borders at 1947

N

0   200 km
0   200 miles

Norwegian Sea

Arctic Circle

NORWAY   SWEDEN   FINLAND

North Sea

Baltic Sea

U.S.S.R.

DENMARK

IRELAND   UNITED KINGDOM

NETHERLANDS

Berlin

BEL.   GERMAN   GERMAN DEMOCRATIC REPUBLIC   POLAND

ATLANTIC OCEAN

FEDERAL REPUBLIC   CZECHOSLOVAKIA

REPUBLIC

FRANCE   SWITZERLAND   AUSTRIA   HUNGARY   ROMANIA

Trieste free state

Black Sea

YUGOSLAVIA   BULGARIA

ANDORRA

Corsica

ITALY   ALBANIA   TURKEY

PORTUGAL   SPAIN

Balearic Is.   *Sardinia*

GREECE   *Aegean Sea*

Crete

Mediterranean

Tangier international   Gibraltar to Britain   to Spain

Sicily

Malta to Britain

Morocco to France   Algeria to France   Tunisia to France   *Sea*

contributed to a terrible famine in 1932–1933, which cost over six million lives.

In the face of possible protest, Stalin conducted the Great Purge of 1936–1938, executing 250,000 supposed "enemies of the people" following charges based on the flimsiest of evidence. Those executed included the remaining members of Lenin's original cabinet and many leaders of the Soviet Red Army, who were tried for being part of a Trotskyite conspiracy to bring down the Soviet Union—the evidence was concocted by Stalin. Millions more people were enslaved in the gulag system of labor camps or forced into internal exile in remote parts of the Soviet Union. In total, 1.7 million died in the atrocious conditions of the gulags, which were particularly terrible in Siberia, where average winter temperatures range from -9°F to -49°F (-23°C to -45°C).

CULT OF PERSONALITY

Despite his growing tyranny, Stalin became a hero to many people in the Soviet Union, not least because he rewrote history to make it appear that he had a greater role in the October Revolution of 1917. He created what became known as a "cult of personality" in which many towns were renamed in his honor, statues of him were erected across the country, and increasingly imperious titles were conferred including "Brilliant Genius of Humanity."

His actions in World War II and its aftermath also increased his status. Early on, Stalin entered into a pact with Hitler, which would allow the Soviet Union to reclaim former territories of the Russian Empire. However, Hitler reneged on the deal—his greatest strategic mistake—and invaded the Soviet Union in 1941. Stalin joined the Allies. His determined desire to defeat Germany came at the cost of 27 million Soviet lives, but this seemed of little importance to him. His personal decisions enabled victory, and he changed the balance of power in Europe at the Potsdam conference in 1945, which reorganized post-war Europe.

During the war, Soviet troops had overrun Poland, the east of Germany, and many states in Eastern Europe; Stalin maintained control over these countries during peacetime, preserving them as Communist countries under the hegemony of the Soviet Union. The Soviet Union was now a superpower to rival the United States, and entered a period,

> *His personal decisions enabled victory, and he changed the balance of power in Europe at the Potsdam conference in 1945, which reorganized post-war Europe.*

Lenin and Stalin, who was a member of Lenin's cabinet.

known as the Cold War, of continual political and military tension with the West. The Eastern Bloc countries became police states, where opposition was wiped out by murder and imprisonment, or squashed by fear. It would take those countries more than 40 years to throw off the shackles of the Stalinist era.

Stalin's personal campaigns against his enemies, both real and imagined, continued apace and his behavior became increasingly paranoid. An anti-Semite, in 1952 he claimed that Russian Jewish doctors were assassinating Soviet leaders, so he had hundreds of Jews executed or sent to the gulags.

He died from a stroke on March 5, 1953. His successor, Nikita Khrushchev, formally denounced him in 1956. There are those within Russia, however, who admire him for his strong leadership, and credit him with the place that Russia now holds within the hierarchy of world superpowers.

Winston Churchill

AS PRIME MINISTER OF BRITAIN DURING WORLD WAR II, CHURCHILL BECAME A NATIONAL HERO. THIS WAS THE CROWNING SUCCESS OF A POLITICAL CAREER FULL OF HIGHS AND LOWS.

Churchill came from a wealthy upper-class family with powerful connections. He was born on November 30, 1874, at Blenheim Palace, the first son of Lord Randolph Churchill. He suffered from a speech defect (not aided in later life by his apparent alcoholism), but he was able to control this problem effectively in the slow delivery of his momentous wartime speeches. He initially joined the army but became a war correspondent in the Boer War, during which he was imprisoned in Pretoria but made a thrilling escape. This was one of the first major escapades in a life that was full of drama.

His political career got off to a shaky start after he became Conservative member of parliament (MP) for Oldham in 1900; never one to hold back on his opinions, he disagreed with party policy and defected to the Liberal party. He held positions in the Liberal government, including home secretary, and received his first taste

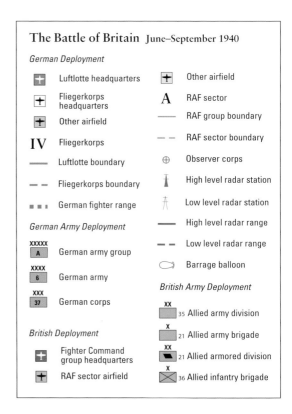

Strategic map of the Battle of Britain.

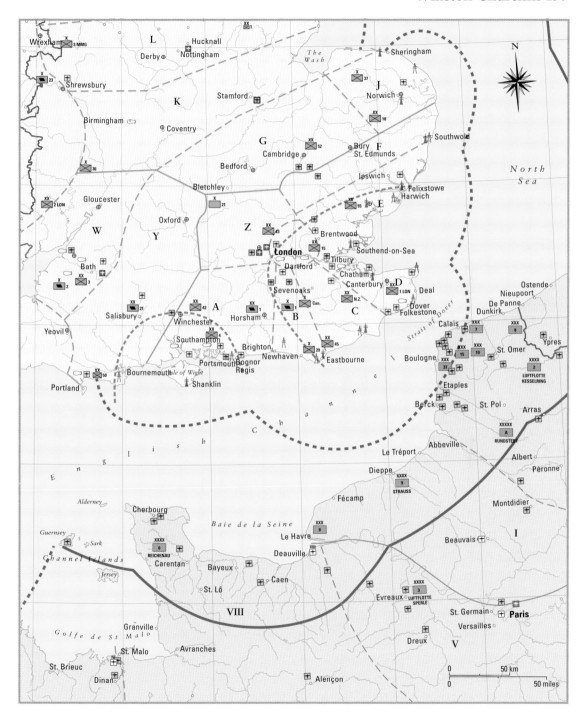

The meeting at Yalta at the end of World War II between Churchill, Roosevelt and Stalin is immortalized in stone.

of military management when he was appointed first lord of the Admiralty in 1911. He resigned due to his responsibility for the ill-fated battle of Gallipoli at the beginning of World War I. He then served in the trenches in France in 1915–1916. Prime Minister Lloyd George made him minister of munitions on his return, and he was particularly concerned with the development of the tank, which he realized would be a crucial weapon in future conflicts. He became secretary for war in 1918–1921, when his sometimes inhumane toughness was revealed in a memorandum recommending the gassing of tribes who rebelled against British control of Mesopotamia. This appointment was followed by an impasse in his career, when he left both parliament and the Liberal party.

FINEST HOURS

In 1924, he returned to parliament as a Conservative MP and became chancellor, but he fell out of favor throughout the 1930s due to further disagreements with Conservative policy on Indian self-rule, rearmament, and appeasement when Adolf Hitler started to threaten Germany's neighboring countries.

War brought out the very best in Churchill. When Britain finally declared war on Germany in 1939, he returned to his post at the Admiralty in Chamberlain's government. When Chamberlain resigned, this difficult firebrand who seemed to enjoy making trouble in peacetime was nevertheless deemed the correct man to lead the country in wartime. In May 1940, with the war going quite badly for Britain, he became prime minister of an all-party government. In a famous speech he accepted the position, saying, 'I have nothing to offer but blood, toil, tears, and sweat...You ask, what is our aim? I can answer in one word: Victory." This was followed by another rousing and famous speech, made in June, when Britain seemed likely to lose the war in France and faced the imminent prospect of German invasion: "We shall fight on the beaches, we shall fight on the landing grounds, we shall fight in the fields and in the streets, we shall fight in the hills; we shall never surrender."

> *We shall fight on the beaches, we shall fight on the landing grounds, we shall fight in the fields and in the streets, we shall fight in the hills; we shall never surrender.*

From July to October 1940, the Battle of Britain was waged, with the German Luftwaffe assaulting Britain in a sustained bombing campaign, aiming to force Britain out of the war and make it ripe for invasion. The Luftwaffe starting bombing ports and shipping convoys, followed by airfields, factories, and the transport infrastructure, and then civilian targets.

The Germans initially thought they could destroy the Royal Air Force in four weeks, but Churchill directed the war effort toward the provision of pilots and planes, including the Spitfire. The airmen fought brilliantly over the course of three months and turned the war in Britain's favor.

Churchill proved his diplomatic skills in meetings with the Allies across the world, particularly with Franklin Roosevelt, the president who brought the United States into the war in December 1941. Churchill agreed the final plans for victory with Stalin and Roosevelt at Yalta in February 1945. The unconditional surrender of Germany was announced in May 1945.

Churchill was a hero, but the populace rejected his Conservative party in the ensuing general election and instead elected the more social welfare-minded Labour party, in the hope that it would quickly restore and improve the fabric of Britain. He became prime minister again in 1951, but resigned in 1955 at the age of 80. At his death in 1965, he was granted the honour of a state funeral. He received a Nobel Prize in 1953, but not for his efforts to bring peace to Europe—the prize was for literature, as he was a gifted historian.

Benito Mussolini

FOR 18 YEARS, HE WAS THE DICTATOR OF ITALY AND GAVE THE WORLD THE TERM
FASCISM. HE CONDUCTED A REIGN OF TERROR AGAINST HIS OPPONENTS AND
SUPPORTED THE NAZIS IN WORLD WAR II BEFORE HIS IGNOBLE DEATH.

Mussolini, born on July 29, 1883, qualified as a teacher before heading to Switzerland to escape military service. Having returned to Italy during an amnesty for deserters, he completed his military service and became involved in the radical left-wing press. However, he was expelled from the Socialist party when he advocated the idea of Italy joining World War I against Germany. He soon shifted to the right, founding the Fascist party in 1919. The Italian word *fascismo* ("political group") was innocent enough, but the party's intentions were not innocent at all. He found support among disillusioned war veterans and formed them into violent squads known as the Blackshirts, who squashed Mussolini's opposition with episodes of remorseless violence and a terrorist campaign against the Socialists. Support within Italy also came from industrialists, landowners, and, importantly, leading figures in the army and police.

In 1921, the Fascists were invited to join the coalition government. Over the course of the next year, Italy slid into a political shambles in the absence of firm rule, and the Blackshirts became the unofficial police authority on the streets. In October 1922, the Blackshirts marched into Rome and Mussolini presented himself as the only man capable of restoring order to the country. The Italian king asked him to become prime minister at the head of a coalition government, but Mussolini was not interested in government by compromise. He started to disassemble the democratic institutions of the country, and in 1925 he became dictator. In the following year, he banned all opposition parties. Over the course of just a few years, *Il Duce* ("the Leader"), as he was now known, had become the only real voice of authority in Italy. An egomaniac, he remodeled the legal, political, and education systems of the country along Fascist lines. Having

Mussolini and Fascist Blackshirts during the march on Rome in 1922.

survived one of several assassination attempts on April 6, 1926, he said to his supporters, "If I advance, follow me; if I retreat, kill me; if I die, avenge me." In time, he would retreat—in fact, he would run for his life—but his enemies killed him and his death was never avenged.

Initially, one of Mussolini's greatest admirers was Adolf Hitler, who copied the Blackshirts with his own Brownshirts and initiated a similarly aggressive campaign in support of Nazism in Germany. Hitler learned from Mussolini that he could still gain popular support despite organizing a bloody, brutal campaign to subdue any opposition. Both leaders also had imperial ambitions beyond their borders. Mussolini believed that Italy should colonize the

Mussolini and Hitler in Munich in June 1940.

whole Mediterranean. He bombarded Corfu into submission in 1923, set up a puppet regime in Albania, and consolidated Italian power in Libya. In 1935–1936, Mussolini invaded Ethiopia, annexing it into his new Italian Empire. He also supported General Franco with military assistance during the Spanish Civil War.

In 1936, with Hitler now chancellor of Germany, the two leaders formed the Axis alliance, and in 1939 made an official agreement of cooperation, the Pact of Steel. Mussolini also followed his protégé's anti-Semitic policies (despite having had a series of affairs with a Jewish author), and introduced legislation to strip Jews of their Italian citizenship and remove them from positions of authority. During all this, Mussolini remained beloved by a large section of the Italian populace. However, as a military leader he was a failure and this—rather than the murders, anti-Semitism, and subversion of democracy—was his undoing.

STRING OF DISASTERS

Having joined the war in 1940, Italy helped the German invasion of France and conquered British Somaliland, adding it to the Italian Empire. However, from 1941 onward, Mussolini's campaign against the Allies resulted in a string of disasters. The Italians were defeated in North Africa (including at El Alamein in 1942), East Africa, the Balkans, and Greece. The Allies then successfully invaded Sicily in July 1943. His support at home disintegrated. He was forced to resign and was imprisoned by his own supporters in the Fascist government, which signed an armistice with the Allies. Hitler, never a lover of personal failure, nonetheless remained loyal to Mussolini. He made advances into northern Italy, and arranged for German parachutists to free Mussolini in September 1943. Mussolini then set up a government in northern Italy, but by this time he was simply Hitler's puppet.

In April 1945, with the Allies continuing to gain ground and advancing northward through Italy, he attempted to flee across the border into neutral Switzerland. Anti-Fascist Italian partisans captured him at Lake Como and shot him. His body was hung upside down in a public square in Milan and was stoned by his former adoring public, an ignoble ending for a violent and, at heart, cowardly leader.

FACT FILE

Benito Mussolini

Born: 29 July 29, 1883

Died: 28 April 28, 1945

Birthplace: Predappio, Italy

Historical Role: Italian politician and leader of the National Fascist Party

Presidency: October 1922–July 1943

Historic Feats: Mussolini founded the Fascist party in 1919; became dictator in 1925; expanded the Italian Empire

Historic Downfalls: Mussolini's campaign against the Allies in World War II produced a string of disasters, causing him to lose the support of Italians

Hero or Villain: Before the war, Mussolini's people considered him a hero. After the war, however, he was exposed as a villain

Adolf Hitler

A VEGETARIAN ARTIST WHO BECAME THE GREATEST VILLAIN OF THE TWENTIETH CENTURY, HITLER WOULD EXTERMINATE SIX MILLION JEWS, WHILE OVER **60** MILLION PEOPLE DIED IN THE WAR CAUSED BY HIS POWER-HUNGRY MANEUVERS.

Hitler was born in Austria on April 20, 1889, and was raised in poverty in Vienna. A failing artist with no qualifications, he moved to Munich and fought as a volunteer in the German army in World War I. He then became a spy on behalf of the German military. In 1919, he infiltrated the extreme German Workers' Party, but this was no quiet undercover agent. Within two years he had become the party's leader, renaming it the Nationalist Socialist German Workers' Party (the Nazi Party for short).

In 1919 he infiltrated the extreme German Workers' Party, but this was no quiet undercover agent. Within two years he had become the party's leader...

The Nazis were fervent right-wing anti-Semites and antiCommunists who believed in the greatness and purity of the German race. In 1923, Hitler led the Nazis in a failed armed uprising and served nine months in jail, using the time to write *Mein Kampf* (*My Struggle*). Undeterred, he returned to politics. Over the next decade, his charismatic persona and extreme views gained popular support in an age of economic and political turmoil. In 1933, he became chancellor of a coalition government. While his Brownshirt supporters terrorized his opponents and minorities on the streets, he removed his political enemies from government, declared that the Nazis were the only legal party and introduced a series of anti-Jewish laws.

EXPANDING GERMAN TERRITORIES
In 1936, Hitler formed an alliance with the Italian dictator Benito Mussolini and began to concentrate on German expansion. The Rhineland, a military-free zone on the border with France since World War I, was reoccupied by German troops. Two years later, in a show of seemingly indomitable

The political map of Europe in 1942; the effects of Hitler's expansionist plans are clearly evident.

Adolph Hitler's life ended in suicide in a Berlin bunker.

WORLD WAR II BEGINS

To begin with, France, Britain, and the other Allies were no match for the German war machine or for Hitler's ruthless strategies. He occupied Denmark and Norway and, in a tactical masterstroke, his army swept through Belgium and into France, north of the main Allied defenses. By June 1940, France had fallen and the British army was forced to evacuate at Dunkirk. However, he lost the Battle of Britain later that year, when he tried to wipe out the British air force prior to a planned invasion.

Otherwise, his master plan did not falter. By 1941, almost every country in Europe and a swathe of North Africa had become part of the German Empire (the Third Reich), one of its Axis, or one of its conquests. Millions of people who did not fit Hitler's ideal of a master race—Jews, Slavs, Romany gypsies, homosexuals, and political opponents—were herded into concentration camps, kept in appalling conditions, starved, made to undertake slave labor, experimented upon, and eventually exterminated.

STRATEGIC ERRORS

Britain, it seemed, stood virtually alone in Europe as a fighting force trying to defy Hitler's dominance. However, Hitler and his Axis soon made two huge strategic

military strength, Hitler's forces took over Austria, followed by the Sudetenland in Czechoslovakia. In March 1939, he annexed the rest of Czechoslovakia. Then in September, having made a pact with Russia, he invaded Poland. France and Britain, having attempted to avoid another world war, finally decided that enough was enough. The bloodiest conflict in the history of the world was underway.

mistakes that would cost them the war. First, Hitler invaded Russia in the summer of 1941. The Soviets had their own ruthless leader in Stalin, as well as massive manpower on their side, and the Germans became involved in a long, attritional resource-sapping war on the Eastern front.

Meanwhile, the United States had sat on the sidelines of the war in Europe until Japan, one of Germany's Axis in Asia, attacked the U.S. naval base at Pearl Harbor in December 1941. A day later, the U.S. declared war on Japan. Germany, according to the terms of its alliance with Japan, in turn, had to declare war on the U.S. This brought the American military powerhouse into the war on the side of the British. Over the next three years, the Russians would force the Germans back in the east, while other Allies made gains in North Africa and Italy.

Then the British, the Americans, and their Allies landed a huge force in France in June 1944. The writing was on the wall for the Third Reich.

NO SURRENDER

High-ranking Nazis turned against Hitler and attempted to assassinate him with a bomb on July 20, 1944. He survived, but the end was nigh. By April 1945, Soviet forces had reached Berlin, while the other Allies approached from the west and south.

Surrender was not an option for Hitler. On April 29, he married his mistress Eva Braun in a Berlin bunker—they would be married for just one day. They committed suicide before they could be captured along with a number of high-ranking Nazis and their families.

FACT FILE

Adolf Hitler

Born: April 20, 1889

Died: April 30, 1945

Birthplace: Braunau am Inn, Austria

Historical Role: German dictator and leader of the National Socialist (Nazi) Party

Marital Alliances: Eva Braun (1945)

Historic Exploits: Became the leader of the extreme German Workers' Party in 1919 and renamed it the Nationalist Socialist German Workers' Party; became chancellor of a coalition government in 1933; took over the Rhineland, Austria, and Czechoslovakia; invaded Poland in 1939 and instigated World War II.

Historic Downfalls: The Germans were defeated and high-ranking Nazis turned against Hitler

Circumstances of Death: Hitler and his wife committed suicide on April 30, 1945

Hero or Villain: Villain

Mao Zedong

BORN IN HUNAN PROVINCE, THIS PEASANT'S SON WAS THE CREATOR OF THE COMMUNIST PEOPLE'S REPUBLIC OF CHINA. HE SET CHINA ON THE ROAD TO BECOMING A MAJOR GLOBAL FORCE, BUT MILLIONS DIED DUE TO HIS POLICIES.

A former library assistant at Beijing University, Mao's real focus was the foundation of Communist ethics in China. He cofounded the Chinese Communist Party (CCP) in 1921 and became its head of propaganda. The Communist party soon formed an alliance with the larger Kuomintang Nationalist party in order to defeat the warlords who held sway over northern China. However, the Kuomintang soon turned against their political rivals, and in 1927 Mao was fired from his position by Kuomintang leader Chiang Kai-shek. Mao and his fellow communists retreated to southeast China and set up a communist republic in Jiangxi in 1931–1934. The Kuomintang were intent on completely suppressing communism and threatened to annihilate the CCP's force, known as the Red Army, in 1934. Mao helped lead the Red Army out of the clutches of the Kuomintang in a 6,000 mile (9,660 km) "Long March," creating a new base at Shaanxi in the northeast.

COMMUNISM PREVAILS

Mao became head of the Chinese Communist Party in 1935. He was forced into another alliance with the Kuomintang in order to repel the Japanese invasion in 1937–1945. After the end of World War II and the defeat of the Japanese, hostilities with the Kuomintang resumed in a full-out civil war. Mao, who was to write more than 2,300 publications in his lifetime, proved himself to be more than an academic theoretician by pursuing guerrilla tactics with his highly mobile

> Mao helped lead the Red Army out of the clutches of the Kuomintang in a 6,000 mile (9,660 km) "Long March," creating a new base at Shaanxi in the northeast.

The Chinese attack during the Korean war.

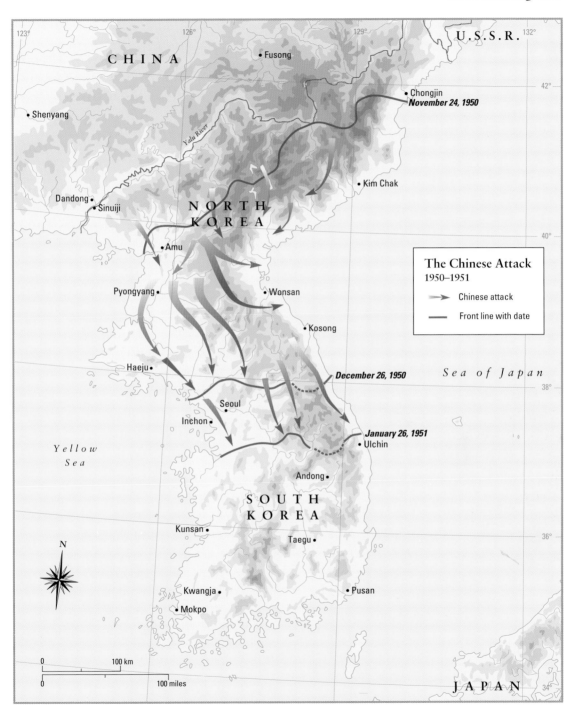

C H I N A

Fusong

U.S.S.R.

Chongjin
November 24, 1950

Shenyang

Yalu River

Kim Chak

Dandong
Sinuiji

N O R T H
K O R E A

Amu

Pyongyang

Wonsan

Kosong

The Chinese Attack
1950–1951

Chinese attack

Front line with date

Haeju

December 26, 1950

Sea of Japan

Seoul

Inchon

January 26, 1951
Ulchin

Yellow
Sea

Andong

S O U T H
K O R E A

Kunsan

Taegu

N

Kwangja

Pusan

Mokpo

0   100 km

0   100 miles

J A P A N

Mao remains an iconic symbol to the Chinese people, and is still revered as an influential figure.

force. He was able to establish the People's Republic of China under his leadership on September 1, 1949, after defeating the Kuomintang at Nanjing—his long-time enemy Chiang Kai-shek fled to Taiwan.

Mao started the quest to remold China into a Communist state by putting industry under state control and reshaping farming into agricultural collectives. He had a strong ally in the form of Kim Il-sung, the leader of Communist North Korea (which in 1948 had divided from capitalist South Korea, with a shared border along the 38th parallel). North Korea had assisted the CCP in the civil war and, when frictions between the two Koreas escalated into warfare in 1950, Mao returned the favor. When the American-led United Nations forces, fighting on behalf of the South, advanced into North Korean territory, China intervened with military force and scored major victories against the Americans in late November. Before the end of December, the Chinese had pushed the U.S. 8th Army right back to the 38th parallel. Alongside the North Koreans, the Chinese then conquered the South Korean capital of Seoul in January 1951. The Korean War ended in stalemate, with the border restored at the 38th parallel, but the United States now knew that the Chinese were a strong military force willing to fight back.

THE CULTURAL REVOLUTION

Mao remained the head of the government until his death in 1976 and was adored by much of the Chinese public. His *Quotations* and *Little Red Book*, in which he revealed how to adapt Communism to Chinese conditions, each sold hundreds of millions of copies, and many of his ideas are still valued to this day.

> *His Quotations and Little Red Book, in which he revealed how to adapt Communism to Chinese conditions, each sold hundreds of millions of copies.*

However, there are two considerable blights on his reputation. The first was the Great Leap Forward in 1958–1960, which was an attempt to mass mobilize the agricultural workforce. It had a devastating effect on output, and proved to be a considerable failure for Mao's economic theory. The second blight was his lack of humanity. The Cultural Revolution of 1966–1969 instigated a wholesale change in Chinese society through the purging of "impurity," such as non-Maoists. In the state-sponsored mass killings and persecutions, there were several different types of victims. Some were set upon by mobs in the street and often forced to commit suicide in public places; unarmed civilians were killed by the Red Army, local militias or security forces in pogroms against "class enemies;" alleged conspirators were tortured to death in political witch hunts; and armed resistors were also executed. Usually the victims had to endure public humiliation, interrogation, torture, and imprisonment before their deaths. Millions died and countless more lived in fear of not just the authorities, but their neighbors. China veered toward anarchy, but Mao persisted with the slaughter and squashed all resistance in the nation.

Deng Xiaoping, the leader of the People's Republic after the death of Mao, formally criticized some of his excessive policies, but like Kim Il-sung in North Korea, Mao remains almost a deity to many of the older generation in China; his image and his writing still command a huge respect in present-day China.

Oskar Schindler

WHILE MILLIONS OF "UNDESIRABLES," ESPECIALLY JEWS, WERE ROUNDED UP TO FACE THE HORRORS OF THE CONCENTRATION CAMPS, INDUSTRIALIST OSKAR SCHINDLER FOUND A WAY TO SAVE HUNDREDS OF JEWS FROM THE DEATH CAMPS.

Schindler was born in Sudetenland in Czechoslovakia in 1908. Like many people in Sudetenland, Schindler regarded himself as German. He even became a member of the Abwehr, the German military intelligence service, and was imprisoned for betraying the Czech state in 1938. He was released when Adolf Hitler annexed Sudetenland later that year to form part of the new German Empire. Schindler is thought to have resumed work for the Abwehr, helping to fake a Polish attack on a German-speaking radio station, which gave Hitler an excuse to attack Poland and precipitated World War II. In 1939, Schindler confirmed his allegiance to Hitler when he became a member of the Nazi Party.

Schindler was an ostentatious character with an eye for business opportunities. Soon after the invasion of Poland in 1939,

He ingratiated himself with the occupying forces, sending expensive gifts and putting on lavish entertainment for those in positions of authority.

Schindler moved to Krakow in the hope that he could profit from the German occupation. He took over the enamelware factory of a bankrupt Jew, and employed 1,000 Jewish workers as cheap labor. The factory was soon manufacturing products to support the German war effort. He ingratiated himself with the occupying forces, sending expensive gifts and putting on lavish entertainment for those in positions of authority. Most Germans in Krakow merely thought that he was a useful cohort and a sympathizer with the Third Reich. However, Schindler was quietly becoming more sympathetic to the plight of the Jews.

COMPASSION FOR THE JEWS

The Germans soon began to carry out their awful mission to "cleanse" the population of Jews. In Krakow, the Jewish population

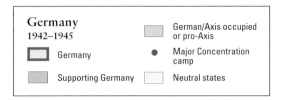

Germany
1942–1945

☐ Germany

▨ Supporting Germany

▨ German/Axis occupied or pro-Axis

● Major Concentration camp

☐ Neutral states

The German empire during the latter part of the Second World War.

Schindler's grave in Israel—the German inscription reads "The unforgettable livesaver of 1200 persecuted Jews."

the raid, and he realized that many more were about to be killed in the camp. He bribed the German authorities to release hundreds of Jewish detainees into his "custody," effectively setting up his factory as a branch of the Plaznow camp. From the German point of view, the Jews were in the custody of a Nazi supporter who was merely using an underclass of people to work as slave labor in his factory. In fact, he was saving their lives. He and his wife Emilie would make sure that his Jewish workers were fed properly and given medical treatment. He would claim that certain workers—including women, children, and the handicapped—were completely essential to his factory, even if they were totally unskilled, and prevented them being taken away to the camps. The Gestapo was suspicious and arrested him on charges of corruption several times, but he was able to use his influence, wealth, and bribery to curtail any further investigation into his affairs.

was forced to live in a ghetto. Families were being plucked out of their homes and sent to concentration camps. Schindler also learny that a supposed Jewish children's home set up by the Germans was, in fact, just a gateway to death—the children were being exterminated.

Schindler's distress grew at the beginning of 1943, when the ghetto was raided and its residents were sent en masse to the Plaznow concentration camp. Some of his own workers were murdered in

THE MOVE TO SUDETENLAND

With the Russians advancing through Poland in 1944, the Germans were slaughtering the camp prisoners in the gas chambers or herding them toward Germany. Schindler knew that he would have to shut down his factory in Poland, and decided to move the enterprise to his home region of Sudetenland.

Incredibly, he convinced the Germans that he should move his Jewish labor force with him. He took 1,100 workers, including 300 women from Auschwitz, and thereby saved them from almost certain death.

By the end of the war, Oskar and Emilie were virtually penniless, having spent their fortune on bribes and on keeping their workers alive. After the war, he and his wife lived in Argentina for a time, hoping to start a new life. However, his attempts to set up new businesses failed, he abandoned his wife, and then died in poverty in 1974 at the age of 66. He was eventually buried in Jerusalem, having said, "My children are here." He was granted an honor by Israel marking him as "Righteous among the Nations"—an honor given to those non-Jews who were responsible for saving the lives of Jews during World War II.

THE STORY EMERGES

The life-saving deeds of this Nazi remained largely unknown until a Jewish survivor named Leopold Pfefferberg met an Australian author Thomas Keneally in a Los Angeles bookshop in the late 1970s. He handed the author Schindler's own handwritten list of the people he had saved from the gas chambers—Pfefferberg himself was number 173 on the list—and asked Keneally to tell Schindler's story.

FACT FILE

Oskar Schindler

Born: April 28, 1908

Died: October 9, 1974

Birthplace: Sudetenland, Czechoslovakia

Historical Role: German industrialist who saved the lives of 1,100 Jews during World War II

Historic Feats: Schindler persuaded German authorities to release hundreds of Jewish detainees into his "custody" during World War II. In 1944, he moved 1,100 people to Sudetenland, saving their lives

Legacy: Schindler's handwritten list of names survived and found its way to the author Thomas Keneally in the late 1970s. His story has since formed the basis of a novel and an Oscar-winning movie

Hero or Villain: Hero

The result was a Booker-prize winning novel that was adapted into the Oscar-winning movie *Schindler's List*, directed by Steven Spielberg in 1993.

Mother Teresa

SHE BECAME A WORLDWIDE SYMBOL OF KINDNESS DURING HER OWN LIFETIME, AS SHE GAVE UP HER LIFE TO CARING FOR THE POOR AND SICK IN INDIA. SOON AFTER HER DEATH, SHE WAS BEATIFIED BY THE ROMAN CATHOLIC CHURCH.

Agnes Gonxha Bojaxhiu was born in Skopje, Macedonia, in 1910. She was an ethnic Albanian but she was to become famous for her work in India where extreme poverty remains an endemic problem. Her family were devout Catholics and at the age of 12, she decided she wanted to become a nun and work in India. At 18, she joined an Irish order of nuns, the Sisters of Loreto, and went to Ireland to learn English, which would become a major tool in her efforts to inform the world of the plight of the poor in Calcutta. She traveled to India in 1929, joining a convent first in Darjeeling and then in Calcutta, where she worked as a teacher. She took the name Teresa after St. Thérèse of Lisieux.

INDIAN CITIZENSHIP

Immediately after World War II, India entered a period of immense internal strife during Independence and Partition, in 1948. The country split along religious lines, with West and East Pakistan becoming new Muslim countries. During this time of violence and discord Mother Teresa received her vocation to live and work with the poor in the slums of Calcutta. She became an Indian citizen in 1948, and two years later set up the Missionaries of Charity, an order of Catholic nuns and brothers who are dedicated to charitable work. Her particular focus was to help the street children of Calcutta living in desperate conditions, but her charity also attempted to provide care and a dignified death to any person, no matter how destitute or diseased. She set up a free hospice in the grounds of a Hindu temple, established a home for abandoned children, and began a refuge for lepers.

GLOBAL RECOGNITION

Her work expanded beyond Calcutta and over the next decades she opened orphanages, hospices, and homes for lepers across India. In 1965, five sisters from the Missionaries of Charity set up a mission in Venezuela, its first operation outside India, and others followed in Italy, Tanzania, and Austria. British journalist Malcolm Muggeridge made a documentary movie about Mother Teresa in 1969, which led to her charitable work gaining greater attention throughout the world as well as sizable donations. More convents and foundations followed in Asia, Europe, Africa, and the United States (where she would be listed first in a Gallup poll of the most admired people of the twentieth century), and the charity added AIDS hospices to its work. There are now more than 600 Missionaries of Charity across the world, with almost 5,000 nuns and 500 brothers working in 120 countries. Mother Teresa traveled the globe to assist victims of famine and disaster, but her own personal possessions were just two saris and a bucket.

A tiny woman with a wizened face in her later years, she remained a familiar figure on television screens, and was awarded the Nobel Peace Prize in 1979.

She died on September 5, 1997. The Catholic Church can sometimes take many centuries to canonize a saint, but in her case the initial steps were undertaken with great speed and she was beatified in 2003. The Church is awaiting evidence that she performed two miracles before it will make her a saint.

A minority of people regard this global symbol of virtue as something of a villain. Some object to the work of Christian missionaries in non-Christian countries, because they try to convert people from their original faith. The sanitation and quality of care in the charity's homes has also been criticized. Others condemn her acceptance of donations and honors from publicity-seeking dictators, such as the Duvalier family of Haiti, who were responsible for atrocities in their own country.

Her ultraconservative views also raised hostility, as she was against contraception and abortion even though the problems of poverty in India are compounded by the vast numbers of unwanted and abandoned children. Other people question the charity's finances—it raises a great deal of money, but has refused investigations into its accounts. All this is a reminder that every hero, even one regarded by most people as a saint, is a villain in the eyes of some other people.

> " *British journalist Malcolm Muggeridge, made a documentary movie about Mother Teresa in 1969, which led to her charitable work gaining greater attention ...* "

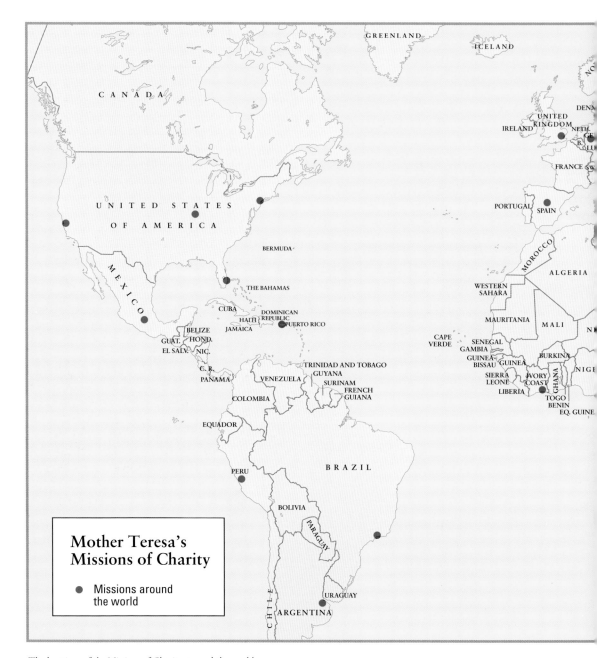

The locations of the Missions of Charity around the world.

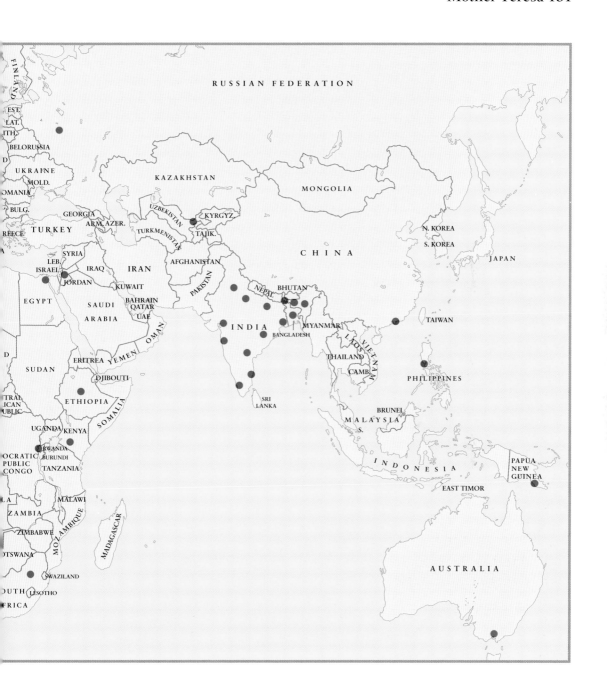

John F. Kennedy

THE GOLDEN BOY OF AMERICAN POLITICS, JFK'S ASSASSINATION HAS PRESERVED HIS REPUTATION DESPITE REVELATIONS OF WOMANIZING AND THE SUSPECTED CORRUPT ACTIVITIES OF HIS POWERFUL FAMILY.

John F. Kennedy will always remain a hero of the civil rights movement, despite criticism regarding alleged financial irregularities amongst his family and his own sexual shenanigans.

His political achievements somewhat pale in comparison to those of other presidents of the United States, and he dragged the country into the Vietnam War. And yet he remains a hero, not least because he had two major assets that at least in the popular imagination, help inure him from criticism—he had effortless charm and he died young.

John Fitzgerald Kennedy, otherwise known as Jack, was born in Brookline, Massachusetts, on May 29, 1917. He was the son of a wealthy Irish-American financier Joseph, who used his power, riches, and connections to help advance the political fortunes of his family. Jack served with distinction in the U.S. Navy in World War II and, after studying at Harvard, entered the House of Representatives in 1946. Six years later he became the senator for Massachusetts.

POLITICAL AMBITION

He was charismatic and attracted to glamour—he married the beautiful socialite Jacqueline Lee Bouvier in 1953—but he was also gaining a reputation as a civil rights campaigner and as a leading internationalist, believing that the often insular United States should play a vital role in world affairs. Highly ambitious, he decided to stand for the presidential election in 1960 despite his youth and religion—a Catholic had never been elected to the White House. He won the Democratic nomination with ease, standing on a ticket for civil rights and social reform, but his battle against Richard Nixon for the presidency proved to be one of the tightest in history. He scraped home and, at the age of 43, he

The Kennedy family with their dogs during a weekend at Hyannisport, in 1963.

was inaugurated in January 1961. In his inaugural speech he challenged his fellow Americans with the words: "Ask not what your country can do for you, but rather what you can do for your country."

SHORT PRESIDENCY

The golden boy would be president for less than three years. Within that time he would become famous throughout the world as a handsome young politician who was trying to bring a fresh approach to politics. He brought many leading intellectuals to Washington, D.C., creating a "Camelot" of talents (including his brother Robert) that would motivate a new generation of political idealists to become

involved in positive political activism—suddenly it looked as if it really was possible to change the world for the better. In truth, the Kennedy administration changed virtually nothing on the domestic front, with the exception of initiating the Civil Rights Bill, which advanced the causes of racial desegregation and equality.

INTERNATIONAL AFFAIRS

Early on in his term of office, his international reputation was knocked by the Bay of Pigs fiasco in April 1961, when the United States tried and failed to overthrow Fidel Castro, the communist president of Cuba. Kennedy's standing was redeemed by his adept, statesman-like

JFK, Jackie, and the Connallys in the presidential limousine seconds before the assassination.

management of the Cuban missile crisis a year later, which averted a nuclear conflict, and he improved relations with the Soviet Union. His personal appearances on two tours of Europe also won him adoration. In Berlin he told the rapt crowd, "*Ich bin ein Berliner,*" which can be taken to mean "I am a jam doughnut" instead of "I am a Berliner," but such incidents only seemed to enhance his reputation.

Nevertheless, his interference in international affairs was to lead to significant trouble for the United States as he dragged his country into the Vietnam War, sending 12,000 military personnel and 300 helicopters to help resist communist interests in southeast Asia in 1962. The United States would not be able fully to extract itself from the war for 13 years, at the cost of 58,000 dead and 300,000 wounded. At home, domestic "affairs" would also blight his reputation, with Marilyn Monroe listed among his many conquests.

THAT DAY IN DALLAS

On November 22, 1963, while being driven through Dallas during a tour of Texas, he was shot in the head and shoulder. He died almost instantly. Lee Harvey Oswald was arrested and protested his innocence, but he himself was shot on November 24, helping to open the door to a range of conspiracy theories about the assassination that continue to this day.

Whoever was responsible for the act, it ensured that JFK would remain an idol—his time in office was too short to become overly mired in the politics of compromise, whereby his youthful visions would have been sullied by the exhausting complexities of the realpolitik. Heads of state from around the world attended his funeral, and his death was accompanied by a shock so thorough that the question "Where were you when you heard that Kennedy was shot?" became a conversational gambit for many years to come.

The Kennedy family would suffer further tragedy when Robert too was assassinated, but Jack remains a symbol of youthful hope and the possibility of change for the better.

FACT FILE

John F. Kennedy

Born: May 29, 1917

Died: November 29, 1963

Birthplace: Brookline, Massachusetts

Historical Role: The thirty-fifth president of the United States

Marital Alliances: Jacqueline Lee Bouvier (1953)

Presidency: January 20, 1961–November 22, 1963

Historic Feats: Kennedy had a fresh approach to US politics. Under his rule, people began to believe in the possibility of changing the world for the better. His adept management of the Cuban missile crisis in 1962 averted a nuclear conflict, and he improved U.S. relations with the Soviet Union

Historic Mistakes: Kennedy's reputation suffered following the Bay of Pigs incident of 1961, and his interference in international affairs resulted in the U.S. being caught up in the Vietnam War for 13 years

Circumstances of Death: Assassinated in Dallas, Texas, November 22, 1963

Hero or Villain: Kennedy will always be remembered as a hero of American politics and civil rights

Idi Amin

IDA AMIN WAS ONE OF THE MOST BRUTAL AND MURDEROUS RULERS IN THE ENTIRE HISTORY OF AFRICA. OVER 300,000 UGANDANS DIED UNDER HIS RULE, WHILE MANY MORE WERE DISPOSSESSED OF THEIR PROPERTY AND FORCED INTO EXILE.

Ida Amin Dada was born in Uganda around 1925. As some claim that his mother was a sorceress, he perhaps had a somewhat unorthodox upbringing that provided an explanation for his unbridled cruelty in adulthood. Poorly educated, he joined the army, which was under British control until Uganda gained independence in 1962. A large, imposing presence, Amin rose up the ranks, while also becoming Uganda's light-heavyweight boxing champion. In 1966, the Prime Minister Milton Obote declared himself the unelected executive president and placed the apparently loyal Amin at the head of the army. Obote's fearsome remorseless henchman squashed his opponents, but soon it Obote's. In 1971, Amin overthrew Obote and set up a military dictatorship.

As some claim that his mother was a sorceress, he perhaps had a somewhat unorthodox upbringing that provided a gateway to his unbridled cruelty in adulthood.

PRESIDENTIAL POWER

His eccentricity and egomania now came to dominate his actions. Insisting on being called "Big Daddy," he had five wives, dozens of mistresses, and fathered more than 30 children. He gave himself the title "His Excellency, President for Life, Field Marshal Al Hadji Doctor Idi Amin Dada, VC, DSO, MC, Lord of All the Beasts of the Earth and Fishes of the Seas, and Conqueror of the British Empire in Africa in General and Uganda in Particular." In 1974, he also anointed himself as the king of Scotland, a country to which he had never been.

Amin set about conducting a reign of terror against his people, including minorities. A convert to Islam, he expelled all Israelis—his former allies—and

The Uganda–Tanzanian war in 1978–1979.

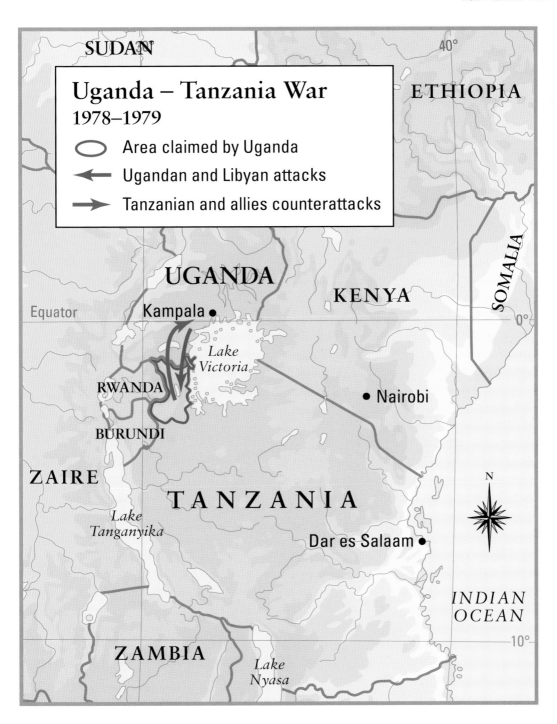

SUDAN

ETHIOPIA

Uganda – Tanzania War
1978–1979

- Area claimed by Uganda
- ← Ugandan and Libyan attacks
- → Tanzanian and allies counterattacks

UGANDA

KENYA

SOMALIA

Equator

Kampala ●

Lake Victoria

0°

RWANDA

● Nairobi

BURUNDI

ZAIRE

TANZANIA

N

Lake Tanganyika

Dar es Salaam ●

ZAMBIA

INDIAN OCEAN

10°

Lake Nyasa

40°

attracted financial support from Muslim countries in order to move Uganda toward becoming an Islamic state.

EXPULSION OF THE ASIANS

The long-established Asian community had become important to the economy of Uganda, but in 1972 Amin also decided to expel all 60,000 British passport-holding Asians, forcing them to leave their property, money, and worldly goods behind. Many went to Britain, where they had to rebuild their lives in poverty.

Perhaps they were the lucky ones. In the course of his eight-year rule, Amin used his infamous, barbaric "killer squads" to murder approximately 300,000 real or imaginary opponents. The squads reveled in torture, while Amin himself is even said to have eaten the flesh of some of his victims. Many Ugandans fled the country, including the Anglican priest John Sentamu who, after receiving a beating on Amin's orders in 1974, escaped to Britain, where he became an archbishop.

INTERNATIONAL CONDEMNATION

Due to the expulsion of the Asians, the corruption of officials, and Amin's personal mismanagement, the economy fell into terrible disarray, while countries including the United States withdrew aid due to the regime's brutality. President Jimmy Carter said that Amin "disgusted the entire civilized world."

Never afraid of such disgust, Amin received international condemnation in 1976 when he was complicit in the Palestinian hijacking of an Air France airplane flying from Tel Aviv to Paris via Athens. The plane was diverted to Uganda's Entebbe airport, and more than a hundred Israeli passengers and crew were held hostage. The hijackers threatened to execute the hostages unless demands for the release of Palestinian prisoners were met, so Israel sent covert special forces into Uganda and conducted a raid on the plane. They killed all seven hijackers and 45 Ugandan troops, rescuing all but four of the hostages.

THE UGANDA–TANZANIA WAR

Despite the chaos and hardship his country was enduring, in 1978 Amin sent troops into northern Tanzania to claim land alongside Lake Victoria. He gained military assistance in this endeavor from another bizarre dangerous dictator, Colonel

> *In the course of his eight-year rule, Amin used his infamous, barbaric 'killer squads' to murder approximately 300,000 real or imaginary opponents.*

Gaddafi of Libya, but in the end the Uganda–Tanzania War would bring about Amin's downfall. In 1979, exiled Ugandan nationalists united with Tanzanian troops in a counterattack that drove right up to the Ugandan capital of Kampala. On April 11, Amin was forced to flee to Libya, where he lived under the protection of Gaddafi, despite the fact that he was wanted to face trial for human rights abuses. His long-term country of residence was Saudi Arabia, which paid him a regular stipend on condition that he kept out of politics.

A RETURN TO UGANDA?

Toward the end of his life, Amin's family showed a shocking disregard for his victims and their families when they asked the Ugandan government to allow him to return home. However, they were told that he would be arrested immediately and tried for his atrocities against the Ugandan people if he reentered the country. This was not an option for Amin—he had never shown any remorse, certainly would never apologize, and had no intention of facing trial. By then, he was suffering from multiple organ failure and fell into a coma in Jeddah, Saudi Arabia, and died on August 16, 2003. He was responsible for unimaginable slaughter, but he had been protected from justice for 24 years.

FACT FILE

Idi Amin

Born: ca. 1925

Died: August 16, 2003

Birthplace: Koboko, Uganda

Historical Role: Third president of Uganda

Presidency: February 2, 1971– April 11, 1979

Historic Exploits: Amin expelled all Israelis and 60,000 British passport-holding Asians from the country; used "killer squads" to murder around 300,000 opponents. Also complicit in the Palestinian hijacking of an Air France plane in 1976, and sent troops into northern Tanzania to claim land

Circumstances of Death: Amin suffered multiple organ failure and fell into a coma. He died in a hospital in Jeddah, Saudi Arabia

Hero or Villain: Villain

Pol Pot

POL POT WAS ONE OF THE GREATEST VILLAINS OF MODERN TIMES AND HIS KHMER ROUGE GOVERNMENT IN CAMBODIA UNDERTOOK THE WHOLESALE GENOCIDE OF THE WESTERN-INFLUENCED, EDUCATED, AND MIDDLE-CLASS POPULACE.

Pol Pot, whose real name was Saloth Sar, was born in Cambodia on May 19, 1925. The country was a French colonial protectorate and Saloth Sar, who came from a relatively wealthy family, was educated at French-speaking schools. He concluded his education in Paris, having won a scholarship to study radio electronics there from 1949. While in France he became associated with Communist politics and, on his return to Cambodia in 1953, he joined a clandestine Communist movement that would become known as the Khmer Rouge. After Cambodian independence from France was granted in 1954, he helped direct opposition against the Cambodian monarch, Norodom Sihanouk. In 1963, having become the party's secretary-general, he created a guerrilla network in remote parts of the country. While there, he became impressed by the locals' self-sufficient, communal living, which he wanted to mirror throughout Cambodia.

> *... he became associated with Communist politics and, on his return to Cambodia in 1953, he joined a clandestine Communist movement that would become known as the Khmer Rouge.*

ASCENDANCY OF THE KHMER ROUGE

Sihanouk was overthrown in 1970, but not by the Khmer Rouge. His own prime minister, the U.S.-backed General Lon Nol, deposed him, and he became Saloth Sar's new target. Civil war ensued, with the Khmer Rouge gradually gaining control over most of the country. Saloth's popularity increased when the United States conducted a mass bombing campaign of Cambodian villages as part of its anti Communist tactics, killing 40,000 people. He finally emerged as victorious after the Khmer Rouge forces

A stone marking the graves of Khmer Rouge victims.

took the capital Phnom Penh in 1975. General Lon Nol, fearing execution, fled the country.

RENAMING AND RESTRUCTURING
Never one to take the "softly, softly" approach, Saloth Sar immediately installed himself as the premier, renamed the country Kampuchea, and announced that the calendar had been reset to "Year Zero." He also renamed himself Pol Pot, short for "*Politique potentielle*," the French translation of a phrase supposedly used

by the Chinese to describe him. He was completely against capitalism and the Western influence on Cambodian life that had arisen during colonial rule. He returned his country to an almost wholly agricultural economic system by forcing all city dwellers to abandon the cities and become farm laborers in communes. Religion, currency, and private ownership of property were outlawed.

This rapid, brutal, and wholesale restructuring of economic society was not the greatest of Pol Pot's crimes. He

Skulls of just some of the millions of Khmer Rouge victims.

committed countless atrocities against his own people, with his Khmer Rouge followers mercilessly exterminating a whole class of professional people who had prospered under colonial rule and become influenced by Western values and education. Former government officials, political opponents, Buddhist monks, Christians, Muslims, and ethnic minorities, including Thai and Chinese, were also slaughtered. Anyone deemed an intellectual was killed—even if their sole crime was wearing glasses or being able to speak a foreign tongue. (Obviously, the French-speaking, foreign literature-reading, highly educated intellectual Pol Pot, who was from an ethnic Chinese background, refrained from eradicating himself.) The merciless purge resulted in the deaths of between 1.5 and 3 million people, out of a total population of under 8 million, in the space of just four years—it is one of the worst genocides committed in the history of humankind. Many were murdered in special detention centers set up by the Khmer Rouge, while others died from starvation or from being worked to death.

THE VIETNAMESE INVASION

In 1979, the Vietnamese invaded Kampuchea in response to border disputes and Khmer Rouge incursions into their territory. Pol Pot was deposed and fled to the jungle region bordering Thailand. He remained at large and continued to lead the Khmer Rouge in both controlling this remote region and in its struggles against the new Vietnamese-backed government in Phnom Penh. Incredibly, the Khmer Rouge received foreign aid—including from the U.S. government—due to international animosity toward the Soviet-backed government in Vietnam. Such support persisted despite continuing revelations of the atrocities conducted by the Khmer Rouge administration in 1975–1979, as highlighted in the 1984 movie *The Killing Fields*. The bodies of more than 1.3 million of its victims were found in 20,000 mass graves.

THE FINAL YEARS

Pol Pot remained a strong influence on the Khmer Rouge even after he resigned from his official party posts in 1989. However, in 1997 an internal power struggle within the Khmer Rouge resulted in his own supporters turning against him. He was denounced at a show trial for murdering his own right-hand man and his family, and sentenced to house arrest. Despite the evidence of his atrocities, toward the end of his life Pol Pot maintained, "My conscience is clear." He died on April 15, 1998, possibly committing suicide after the Khmer Rouge agreed to hand him over to face an international tribunal.

> *The merciless purge resulted in the deaths of between 1.5 and 3 million people, out of a total population of under 8 million, in the space of just four years*

FACT FILE

Pol Pot

Born: May 19, 1925

Died: April 15, 1998

Birthplace: Kompong Thom province, Cambodia

Historical Role: Leader of the Khmer Rouge

Historic Exploits: Pol Pot committed one of the worst genocides of all time, killing between 1.5 and 3 million people

Circumstances of Death: He may have committed suicide after the Khmer Rouge agreed to hand him over to an international tribunal

Hero or Villain: Villain

Che Guevara

ONE OF THE WORLD'S MOST FAMOUS REVOLUTIONARY PINUPS, BELOVED OF LEFT-WING STUDENTS, CHE GUEVARA'S IMAGE ADORNED THE WALLS OF STUDENT DORMS FOR GENERATIONS AFTER HIS PREMATURE DEATH.

Ernesto Guevara de la Serna, known as Che, was born in Rosario, Argentina on June 14, 1928. He trained as a doctor, and could have taken the option to lead a quiet, professional life. However, he was not interested in saving lives one by one; he was determined to save the whole world from what he perceived as political injustice.

Guevara left the country to become, for the remainder of his life, a major thorn in the side of US foreign policy against left-wing governments.

While at university, he traveled throughout Central and South America and witnessed the depth of poverty and oppression endured by millions. He was a Marxist who believed that capitalism was responsible for the suppression of the working classes, and deduced that the problems he encountered could only be solved by armed revolution.

No admirer of Juan Perón, the president of his homeland who had been a fascist sympathizer during World War II, Guevara moved to Guatemala in 1953 and became a supporter of the elected president Jacobo Árbenz. When the CIA sponsored a coup that ousted Árbenz due to his Communist connections, Guevara left the country to become, for the remainder of his life, a major thorn in the side of U.S. foreign policy against left-wing governments, particularly in Latin and South America.

REVOLUTION IN CUBA

Guevara reemerged on the Caribbean island of Cuba in 1956, helping to lead the revolution that put in place the communist leader Fidel Castro. Guevara had met Castro in Mexico in 1954 and found him to be sympathetic to his Marxist revolutionary views. With the exception of Fidel and his brother Raúl, the young

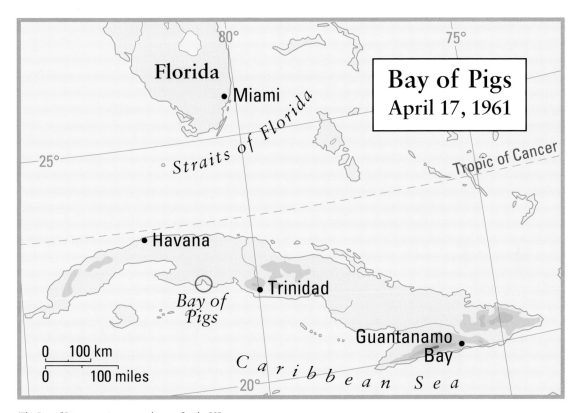

The Bay of Pigs campaign was a disaster for the US.

Guevara was the most important figure of the Cuban revolution. In particular, he was prominent in the guerrilla campaign against the incumbent Cuban dictator Fulgencio Batista. Castro deposed Batista in 1959, and assumed control of the country with Guevara at his side. Guevara became president of the national bank and then minister for industry—perhaps uncomfortable roles for a militant activist, but he helped shape the future of Cuba by persuading Castro to maintain an anti

American stance and shifting him toward an alliance with the Soviet Union.

THE BAY OF PIGS

Because Cuba lies just off the southern tip of Florida, the U.S. government was deeply concerned that a communist regime had been set up so close to home. In 1961, one of the first actions of the new president John F. Kennedy was to sanction an armed raid on Cuba, with the intention of deposing Castro. Aided by air support and attacks on Cuban airfields, 1,200 Cuban exiles trained by the CIA landed in the Bay of Pigs on the southern shore of the island, principally at Playa Girón. The United States thought that the Cuban people would immediately rise up against their new dictator, but, in fact, many Cubans, stirred into action by Guevara, joined the Cuban militia to oppose the invaders. The attempted invasion was an embarrassing failure, and the U.S.-backed force withdrew. Guevara then sent Kennedy a note saying, "Thanks for Playa Girón. Before the invasion, the revolution was weak. Now it's stronger than ever."

> *... Guevara's trademark long hair, beard, and beret ... were captured in an Alberto Korda photograph that became one of the most famous images of the twentieth century.*

Guevara thought that he had helped establish a brave new world of equality, unaware that in time Castro's dictatorial version of Marxism would become regarded as somewhat tortured, ineffectual, and compromised by his own ego.

FURTHER UPRISINGS

In any case, Guevara was not content. The globe-trotting revolutionary left Cuba in 1965 to pursue his goal of inspiring revolution in the developing world. He shifted his focus to Africa, where he fought against white mercenaries employed by the Congolese government and helped train the rebel forces in guerrilla warfare. The uprising was a failure, however, and Guevara briefly returned to Cuba.

His last port of call was Bolivia, named after the greatest revolutionary of the previous century, Simón Bolívar. There, he attempted to lead a peasant uprising against the government of René Barrientos Ortuño. U.S.-backed forces managed to capture Guevara, and he was executed on October 9, 1967. His body was interred in a secret location, but his remains were discovered 30 years later and reburied with honor in Cuba.

In 1960, Guevara's trademark long hair, beard, and beret, with a single star at the front, were captured in an Alberto Korda photograph that became one of the most iconic images of the twentieth century. He has remained the archetypal counter cultural hero, inspiring generations of young idealists who want to move society away from what they consider to be the politics of greed; in contrast, he is reviled by anti Communists.

In truth, Guevara would probably have been disappointed by his achievements in the long-term—Cuba never became a

This image became one of the most iconic symbols of the twentieth century, with posters adorning the walls of millions of students.

FACT FILE

Che Guevara

Born: June 14, 1928

Died: October 9, 1967

Birthplace: Rosario, Argentina

Historical Role: Guerrilla tactician and prominent figure in the Cuban Revolution

Historic Feats: Guevara helped to bring Fidel Castro to power in 1956, and stirred many Cubans to deter the invaders at the Bay of Pigs in 1961

Hero or Villain: Inspirational hero for left-wing idealists

true Marxist utopia, and his attempted uprisings in the Congo and Bolivia failed—but he will continue to be revered as a hero by many because he was a martyr to his ideals.

Martin Luther King Jr.

ONE OF THE GREATEST ORATORS IN THE HISTORY OF THE UNITED STATES, CIVIL RIGHTS CAMPAIGNER AND BLACK LEADER MARTIN LUTHER KING JR. CERTAINLY HAD A CAUSE FOR WHICH IT WAS WORTH SPEAKING OUT.

King helped shift his country toward policies of racial equality and integration by mobilizing sympathisers in mass demonstrations, while always preaching a policy of nonviolence. He paid the ultimate price for his intensive efforts—he was gunned down by an assassin at the age of 39.

Preaching was in Martin Luther King Jr.'s blood. He was born in Atlanta, Georgia, on January 15, 1929, the son and grandson of pastors of the Ebenezer Baptist Church, and followed in his forefathers' footsteps. He became a Baptist pastor in Montgomery, Alabama, in 1954 and became copastor of the Ebenezer Baptist Church in 1960. By then, he was already using his great oratorical skills to preach to a wider audience than Baptist church congregations, and speaking on social instead of purely religious issues.

He was appalled by the continued segregation of American society, particularly in the Southern states, where there were whites-only facilities ranging from schools and libraries to buses and hospitals, movie theaters, restaurants, and bars. There was also a history of lynchings of black people by the Klu Klux Klan, with the local authorities sometimes complicit in murders or related cover-ups.

A committee member of the National Association for the Advancement of Colored People, King came to national attention when he led a bus boycott in Montgomery, Alabama in 1955, the first great black demonstration since World War II. The boycott lasted a year, during which time King was abused and arrested, and his house was bombed, but his endurance paid off— the Supreme Court ruled that segregation on buses was unconstitutional.

FURTHER CIVIL RIGHTS ACTIVISM

In 1957, he formed the Southern Christian Leadership Conference to assist the civil rights movement. Over the next decade, King became a leading public figure in the

Race Riots and Nonviolent Demonstrations
1865–1968

❋ Site of major race riot with dates

Major nonviolent demonstrations

★ Sit-ins organized by Student Nonviolent Coordinating Committee

● Other events organized by SNCC

▨ State with major SNCC Chapter

The spread of race riots and demonstrations across America over the course of a century.

United States and across the world, traveling many thousands of miles, giving 2,500 speeches, and helping to arrange protests against racial discrimination. Despite maintaining his policy of nonviolence, he was arrested more than 20 times and physically assaulted on several occasions. One of his greatest achievements was the Great March on Washington, D.C., on August 28, 1963. Along with other campaigners, he organized a mass gathering of more than 200,000 people, who marched from the Washington Monument to the Lincoln Memorial, reinforcing the connection of the civil rights movement to the causes of the two men most associated with the Wars of Independence and the abolition of slavery. The march concluded with a rousing speech by Martin Luther King Jr., which has become one of the most famous speeches in history: "I have a dream...I have a dream that one day my four little children will live in a nation where they will not be judged by the color of their skin but by the content of their character." The march put the civil rights movement on a new footing. The Student Nonviolent Coordinating Committee, led by Stokely Carmichael, had played a leading role in the march and continued to gain support through organized sit-ins and other events across the Southern states. President Kennedy, a supporter of the movement, now knew that there was enough momentum to start the process of pushing civil rights legislation through Congress.

King was named "Man of the Year" by *Time* magazine and in 1964, at the age of just 35, he became the youngest person to receive the Nobel Peace Prize. By then, Kennedy had been assassinated, but the path had already been laid and President Lyndon B. Johnson made sure that the Civil Rights Act, outlawing major forms of racial discrimination and segregation, became law in July 1964.

OPPOSITION

King was not without critics and enemies, and not only from within the deeply conservative South or the ranks of white supremacists, such as the Ku Klux Klan. His moderate, nonviolent approach was criticized by more militant factions of the Black Power movement, including Malcolm X, Stokely Carmichael, and the Black Panther Party. J. Edgar Hoover, the head of the Federal Bureau of Investigation (FBI), also had King investigated to see whether his authority could be undermined. On April 4, 1968, King was assassinated on the balcony of his motel room in Memphis, Tennessee, where he was preparing to assist a protest by striking garbage-disposal workers. The white supremacist James Earl Ray confessed to the crime, but his rapid retraction and the paucity of evidence against him have led to conspiracy theorists pointing the finger at the FBI, the CIA, or the Mafia.

> *President Kennedy, a supporter of the movement, now knew that there was enough momentum to start the process of pushing civil rights legislation through Congress.*

Martin Luther King's birthday is celebrated as a national holiday in the United States.

LEGACY

Despite his premature death, Martin Luther King Jr. achieved wholesale change through mass mobilization and the power of his oration, and he is remembered as one of history's greatest advocates of civil rights. His birthday is celebrated as a public holiday in the United States on the third Monday of every January, an honor that would have been impossible to foresee when he first took to a podium in the 1955 Montgomery bus boycott.

CONTEMPORARY
WORLD

Due to mass communication and electronic media, the world has become an increasingly smaller place when it comes to tracking conflicts and wars, people and politics. The twenty-first century has spawned a number of hot spots and crises that have thrown up a cast of noteworthy villains and heroes. One hero universally admired for his stance on peace and reconciliation is South Africa's elder statesman Nelson Mandela. However, it seems that for every hero our century has fostered, at least three villains have emerged. Three of the most notorious were Libya's leader Colonel Gaddafi, Iraq's leader Saddam Hussein, and terrorist al-Qaeda leader Osama bin Laden – all of whom have met violent and bloody ends.

Nelson Mandela

IMPRISONED FOR 27 YEARS, NELSON MANDELA BECAME HIS COUNTRY'S FIRST BLACK PRESIDENT. A REVERED STATESMAN, HE HAS CAMPAIGNED FOR PEACE ACROSS THE GLOBE, BECOMING ONE OF THE TRUE HEROES OF THE CONTEMPORARY WORLD.

Nelson Mandela was born with the first name Rolihlahla on 18 July 1918 in the eastern Cape of South Africa and was a member of the Xhosa-speaking Thembu people. Southern Africa had long been controlled by white colonial interests, and the Republic of South Africa was riven by apartheid, a policy of the government of South Africa through which the black majority were treated as second-class citizens, denied full rights and subjected to segregation.

EARLY ACHIEVEMENTS

Rolihlahla, which means 'troublemaker', acquired the English name of Nelson, after the British admiral, from a teacher at school. The two names capture the path of Mandela's career, from scourge of the white government to national hero.

As a young man Mandela joined the African National Congress (ANC), which was attempting to throw off the yoke of apartheid and its white advocates; he set up the ANC Youth League. In the meantime, he qualified as a lawyer and set up a practice in Johannesburg with Oliver Tambo. Mandela and 155 other ANC activists, often painted as terrorists by the white National Party, were arrested in December 1956 and charged with high treason; the resulting trial took four years but every single defendant was acquitted. In 1958 while still awaiting trial, Mandela married Winnie Madikizela, who would later help lead the global campaign for his eventual release from Robben Island.

Racial tensions grew in this period as ANC activists gained momentum in their anti-apartheid campaign, and were spurred on to further action in 1960 when the police massacred 69 black people in Sharpsville. As a result, the ANC, with Mandela now its vice-president, moved beyond its policy of non-violence and started a campaign of military and economic sabotage in order to damage the whites-only government.

Nelson Mandela is one the the world's best-loved figures.

IMPRISONMENT

Mandela was arrested again in August 1962 and later charged with sabotage and attempting to overthrow the government. He defended himself in court, announcing that 'the ideal of a democratic and free society in which all persons live together in harmony and with equal opportunities' was 'an ideal for which I am prepared to die'. He was spared the death penalty and sentenced to life in prison on Robben Island, where he remained for the next 18 years. He was not allowed to leave prison even to attend the funerals of his mother and his son. The ANC continued to oppose apartheid in his absence, while Mandela became the leading symbol of the unjust state. Black youths in the townships rose up in protest against apartheid, leading to thousands of children being murdered or injured. The international community became increasingly disgusted by the actions of the white regime, and mounted boycotts of South African products and sports teams, including the all-white 'Springboks' national rugby team.

In 1980, Oliver Tambo started an international campaign specifically aimed at the release of Mandela, who was transferred to Pollsmoor Prison on the mainland in 1982. 'Free Nelson Mandela' became a popular slogan chanted at protests throughout the world.

The release of Mandela...this single act served to announce that apartheid was dying and that a new, multi-racial democracy in South Africa would be born.

A NEW SOUTH AFRICA

The campaigns and sanctions took their toll on successive all-white South African governments to the extent that President F. W. de Klerk finally lifted the ban on the ANC and freed Nelson Mandela on 11 February 1990. The release of Mandela was televised live across the world and watched by a huge audience – this single act served to announce that apartheid was dying and that a new, multi-racial democracy in South Africa would be born. Mandela soon suffered a personal setback when he and Winnie divorced in 1992, following revelations about her involvement in a series of scandals.

However, the major highlights of his public life soon followed. He and de Klerk were jointly awarded the Nobel Peace Prize in 1993 and, in 1994 the 75-year-old Mandela was overwhelmingly voted in as president of South Africa in the first-ever multi-racial democratic elections in the nation's history.

With Mandela spearheading the country, international trade and sporting events returned to South Africa, and he presided over the 1995 Rugby World Cup, won by the Springboks, and their victory became a symbol of black and white reconciliation. Investors and international companies were attracted back to the country, and while its monumental problems of slums, poverty and a high crime rate continued, South Africa was able to return to a surer economic footing.

AN INTERNATIONAL PEACEMAKER

Mandela, who never showed great animosity to his former captors and preferred to concentrate on reconciliation, left the presidency in 1999. He is known for his graciousness and gentle wit, as well as being one of the greatest statesmen of the modern era. He continued to travel the world to aid peace negotiations in several African conflicts, and created his own charitable foundation. In recent years his work has been curtailed by illness and he retired from public life in 2004, but he remains an international symbol of forbearance, peace and forgiveness.

FACT FILE

Nelson Mandela

Born: July 18, 1918

Birthplace: Umtata, Cape of Good Hope, South Africa

Historical Role: Nationalist campaigner and first black president of South Africa (1994–1999)

Marital Alliances: Evelyn Ntoko Mase (1944–1957); Winnie Madikizela (1957–1992); Graça Machel (1998–present)

Historic Feats: Joined the African National Congress (ANC) and set up the ANC Youth League; joint winner of the Nobel Peace Prize in 1993; became president in 1994. Under his leadership, international trade and sporting events returned to South Africa, and the country returned to a surer economic footing

Hero or Villain: Hero

Saddam Hussein

ONE OF THE MOST BRUTAL DICTATORS OF THE CONTEMPORARY WORLD, SADDAM WAS RESPONSIBLE FOR MANY CRIMES OF CRUELTY AND AGGRESSION AGAINST HIS OWN PEOPLE AND SURROUNDING COUNTRIES.

Saddam Hussein Abd al-Majid al-Tikriti was born in humble circumstances in a mud hut near Tikrit on 28 April 1937. His father disappeared before his birth, so he was initially raised in the household of his maternal uncle. After school, he studied law but left to concentrate his efforts on behalf of the Ba'Arth Party, a pan-Arabic revolutionary group.

SADDAM'S RISE TO POWER

At the time, Iraq was ruled by King Faisal II, who was deposed in 1958 in a military coup by General Abd al-Karim Qasim. In turn, he was overthrown by a coalition of interests, including the Ba'Arthists, in 1963 – but the new president, Abdul Salam Arif, turned against the party and had Saddam imprisoned in 1964. He escaped prison and in 1968 helped lead a successful coup to oust Arif, becoming the right-hand man of President Ahmed Hassan al-Bakr. Over the next decade, as al-Bakr's health

waned, Saddam became the effective power in Iraq; the die was cast for his authoritarian, merciless dictatorship long before he officially became president when he ousted al-Bakr in 1979. He developed a brutal security force, and nationalized oil, banking and other major industries under his personal control. A member of the Sunni Muslim minority, who made up only one-fifth of the population of Iraq, he filled positions of power with Sunnis, relatives and Tikritis so that he could have a stranglehold on the entire country and bend it – by force – to his will.

ERADICATION OF OPPOSITION

As soon as he became president, Saddam ruthlessly exterminated all opposition in the Ba'Arthist Party. He had hundreds of leading members of the party arrested and executed on trumped-up charges of conspiracy, while forcing other high-ranking officials to show their loyalty by forming the firing squads. He then turned

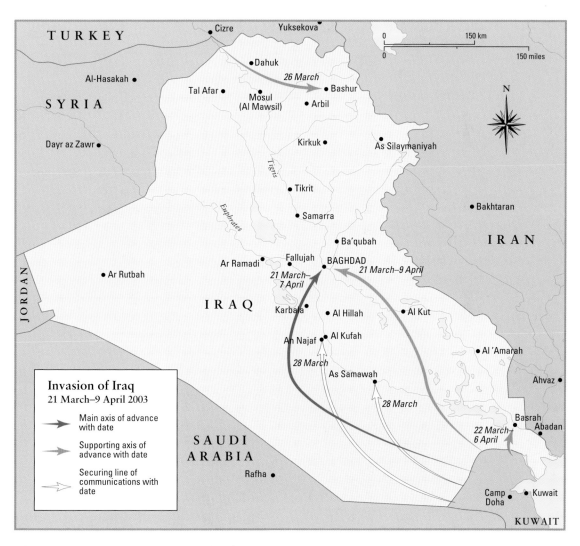

The invasion of Iraq led eventually to Saddam's downfall.

Saddam speaking at a pre-trial hearing.

in a genocidal campaign in which up to 200,000 people were slaughtered. Real, perceived and imaginary foes were also imprisoned, tortured and murdered by the security forces, with hundreds of thousands of people 'disappearing' or executed during the course of his dictatorship. Like many of the world's most evil tyrants, Saddam lived in fear of conspiracies; he even took to having lookalikes pretend to be him at public functions so that potential assassins would hit the wrong target.

THE GULF WAR

Saddam's continued aggression towards neighbouring countries brought him into direct conflict with the West, which eventually led to his downfall. In August 1990, claiming to represent pan-Arabic interests against Western sympathizers, he invaded the oil-rich country of Kuwait and incorporated it into Iraq. The West responded, and the Gulf War began in January 1991 following a United Nations Security Council resolution giving Saddam a deadline for withdrawal. A US-led coalition easily forced the Iraqi army out of Kuwait and drove it northwards in the following month, taking over 175,000 prisoners. There was an opportunity for the coalition to push all the way to the Iraq capital of Baghdad and assist Iraqi rebel forces, who had seized the

his attention to neighbouring Iran. Saddam wanted to be the major power in the region and invaded the Shia'a-dominated country in 1980, starting a futile war that would cost about half a million lives and last for eight years.

Saddam's viciousness also came to the fore in the suppression of Shia'a Muslims and Kurds within his own borders. In the late 1980s, Kurds and other ethnic minorities in northern Iraq were terrorized opportunity to try to overthrow Saddam. The decision to defer would haunt later U.S. administrations. Saddam brokered for peace and, as part of the cease-fire agreement, agreed to scrap all chemical weapons. The coalition withdrew, leaving the rebel Iraqis at the mercy of Saddam. As usual, no mercy was forthcoming and Saddam killed approximately 100,000 rebels in a bloodthirsty reprisal.

THE IRAQ WAR

Saddam's belligerence and threats in both national and international arenas made him an ongoing enemy of the West, which was continually concerned that impressive oil resources and weaponry were in the hands of such an egomaniacal and callous aggressor. When he refused to allow UN inspectors access to suspected chemical weapons development sites, the coalition, led by the U.S. and Britain, decided to seek a permanent solution to the enduring problem of Saddam. President George W. Bush and Prime Minister Tony Blair claimed to have evidence that Saddam had "weapons of mass destruction" and sent a coalition force into Iraq in March 2003. Iraq soon fell, but the prime target, Saddam himself, escaped until he was found, bearded and disheveled, hiding in a bunker in the following December. He was handed over to the new Iraqi authorities, tried, and hanged on December 30, 2006.

The toll of the Iraq War would be a stain on the reputations of both Bush and Blair as no weapons of mass destruction would ever be found. The rebuilding of Iraq in Saddam's absence would cost many lives as well as years of hardship and unrest, and the coalition forces continued to occupy Iraq for many years after the war was over.

FACT FILE

Saddam Hussein

Born: April 28, 1937

Died: December 30, 2006

Birthplace: Al-Awja, Tikrit

Historical Role: Tyrannical Iraqi prime minister

Historical Exploits: Saddam exterminated all opposition in the Ba'Arthist Party and invaded Iran in 1980, starting a futile war. In the late 1980s, Saddam killed up to 200,000 Kurds and other ethnic minorities in northern Iraq, and invaded Kuwait in 1990

Circumstances of Death: Saddam was tried and hanged by the Iraqi authorities on December 30, 2006

Hero or Villain: Villain

Muammar Gaddafi

HIGHLY ECCENTRIC, AND POSSIBLY BORDERING ON THE INSANE, MUAMMAR GADDAFI RULED LIBYA FOR 42 YEARS, DESPITE ERRATIC POLICIES COMBINING SUPPORT FOR INTERNATIONAL TERRORISM WITH OVERTURES TO THE WEST.

Fear is the greatest weapon in the hands of despots, and Gaddafi knew how to use it to bolster his regime. In the end he was overthrown and killed by his own people during the Arab Spring uprisings of 2011.

Gaddafi was born in June 1942 near Sirte on the coast of Libya. When he was a boy, two of his cousins were killed, and he was wounded, by a mine left by the Italian army during its occupation of Libya in the early twentieth century. The experience set the young Gaddafi against colonial and Western interests in his homeland. He was also a lifetime opponent of Israel, taking part in anti-Israeli protests from the age of 14.

Even as a cadet, he plotted to overthrow the Libyan monarchy, and wanted to lead a strong, militarist Arab country in defiance of Israel...

THE END OF THE MONARCHY

He studied at a military academy in Libya and also received training in Britain during his army career. Although he and the rest of the world referred to him as Colonel Gaddafi, he only graduated to the rank of lieutenant. Even as a cadet, he plotted to overthrow the Libyan monarchy, and wanted to lead a strong, militarist Arab country in defiance of Israel, which had belittled its Arab neighbours in the Six Days' War of 1967. Gaddafi and a group of junior military officers seized their opportunity in 1969 when King Idris was out of the country undergoing medical treatment. Gaddafi led a bloodless coup, abolishing the monarchy and proclaimed the country as the new Libyan Arab Republic.

Gaddafi immediately started to undermine international interests in Libya, shutting down US and UK military bases and forcing international oil companies

Libya's geographical position in North Africa.

to share their profits with the new government. Oil is the region's greatest natural resource and Gaddafi was wise enough to know that it would enable the creation of a new, powerful Libya. From one perspective, Gaddafi was a great leader, making Libya a far wealthier country with better infrastructure, improved education and healthcare, and equal rights across the genders and races. From another perspective, he was an irrational, self-obsessed, murderous tyrant who went out of his way to provoke international conflict and turn his own citizens against each other.

PERSECUTIONS AND INVASIONS

Dissent against Gaddafi was made illegal in 1973 and many people became spies, informing on neighbours and colleagues, which spread a climate of fear throughout the country. Gaddafi was against Islamic fundamentalism, and personally presided over executions of extremists in the 1970s, but he was just as set against proponents of Western-style liberalism. In the 1980s political opponents and critics were mutilated and executed in public, while Gaddafi also sent secret agents abroad to assassinate Libyan dissidents who spoke out against his regime.

> *Oil is the region's greatest natural resource and Gaddafi was wise enough to know that it would enable the creation of a new, powerful Libya.*

Closer to home, he railed against the non-Arab Berber culture in Libya, banning the Berber language and forcing them out of their traditional dwellings. He was also heavily involved in trying to make North Africa and parts of the Middle East a single Arab state, sending forces into Egypt in 1977 when it disagreed with his aggressive policy towards Israel. When President Sadat of Egypt died in 1981, Gaddafi declared a Libyan national holiday. He also sent forces into Sudan and Chad, but suffered a humiliating defeat against the latter in 1987.

TERRORISM AND SUPPORT

Gaddafi was linked with state-sponsored terrorism throughout his dictatorship. He funded terrorist groups in the Far East, and supplied weapons to the Irish Republican Army for its bombing campaign in the UK. In 1984, when protestors gathered outside the Libyan Embassy in London after the execution of two dissidents, his diplomats opened fire and killed a British policewoman. Two years later, Libyan agents exploded a bomb in a nightclub in West Berlin as part of Gaddafi's campaign against Western interests. Then in 1988 agents planted a bomb on a Pan-Am flight supporters on the continent, and was even given the title 'King of Kings of Africa' by fellow rulers.

Despite all this, the main Western powers accepted overtures from Gaddafi in his later years as he appeared to repent his terrorist past and was willing to enter into stronger trade relationships. Perhaps most significantly, he continued to be an opponent of Islamic extremism.

THE END OF A TYRANT

However, when the Libyan people rose up against their leader, having suffered 40 years of atrocities and the suppression of all opposition, the West saw the opportunity to be rid of him. Gaddafi's response to the popular uprising was brutal, killing civilians by using air strikes against rebel towns. Consequently, the United Nations declared a no-fly zone over Libya to protect innocent civilians, and NATO jets bombarded military targets. This helped Libyan rebels to gain the upper hand against the army and take control of much of the country, including Tripoli.

Gaddafi was forced to flee to his hometown of Sirte. On 20 October 2011, the King of Kings of Africa was found hiding in a drain and was shot dead before he could be brought to trial.

Colonel Gaddafi was an opponent of Islamic extremism.

from London to New York, killing all 259 people on board. Gaddafi was also associated with several ruthless African dictators, including Idi Amin, whom he sheltered from justice after he was deposed in Uganda. In turn, he had many

Osama bin Laden

THE MOST WANTED MAN IN THE WORLD
AFTER 9/11, HE WOULD EVADE CAPTURE
FOR YEARS AND, AFTER HIS DEATH, LEFT
BEHIND A NETWORK OF DISCIPLES TO
CONTINUE HIS JIHADIST INTENTIONS.

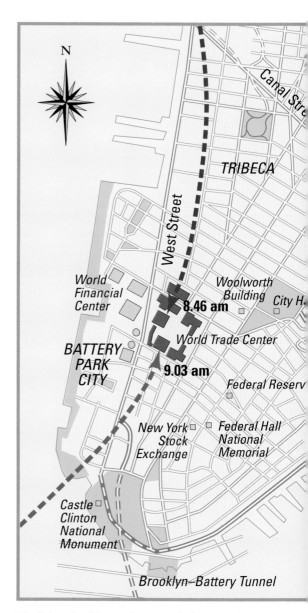

The flight paths of the two planes over Manhattan on 9/11.

One of the 50 children of a Saudi construction billionaire, bin Laden started to turn his back on the comforts of wealth while still a boy. He was an excellent student and became influenced by a teacher sympathetic to the Brotherhood, a sect that sought to have the whole Arabic world controlled by Islamic law and that was willing to pursue extreme, violent measures to fulfil its goal. He was already growing the long untrimmed beard that would help make him immediately recognizable throughout the world.

TRAINING JIHADIST GUERRILLA FIGHTERS
He attended university, but from 1979 onwards his endeavours would be directed towards pro-Islamist activities, including *jihad* – the war or struggle against unbelievers. When the Soviet

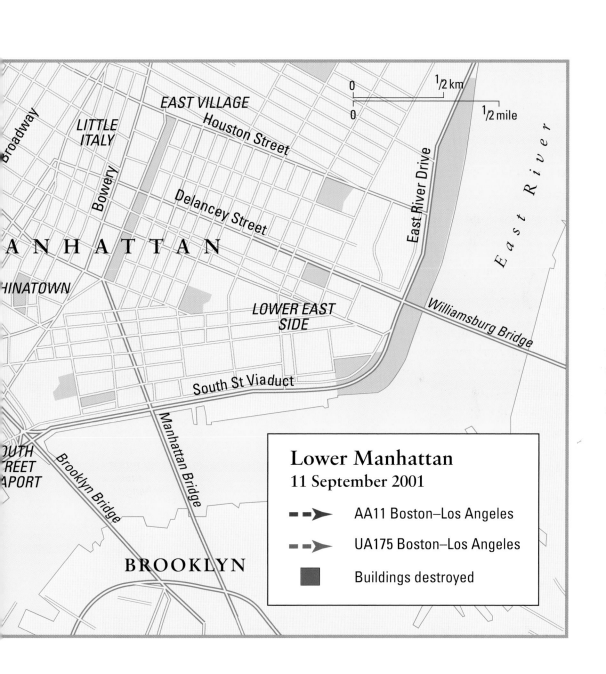

EAST VILLAGE
LITTLE ITALY
Broadway
Houston Street
Bowery
Delancey Street
East River Drive
East River
ANHATTAN
HINATOWN
LOWER EAST SIDE
Williamsburg Bridge
South St Viaduct
JUTH REET APORT
Brooklyn Bridge
Manhattan Bridge
BROOKLYN

0 ——— 1/2 km
0 ——— 1/2 mile

Lower Manhattan
11 September 2001

- - ➤ AA11 Boston–Los Angeles

- - ➤ UA175 Boston–Los Angeles

■ Buildings destroyed

Union invaded Afghanistan in that year, he relocated to Peshawar to help lead the military resistance in the country. With American financial backing, he trained the *mujahedeen*, a group of jihadist guerrilla fighters that would defy the Soviets until their withdrawal from Afghanistan in 1989. Bin Laden returned to Saudi Arabia as a hero and was regarded as a 'freedom fighter' in the United States. However, he was appalled by the corruption of the Saudi government and disgusted that it allowed the US to use what he regarded as sacred Islamic soil as a base in the 1990–1991 Gulf War against Saddam Hussein of Iraq.

Deemed to be one of the biggest threats to US security, he was already a wanted man and had often railed publicly against the West, declaring a holy war against America

AL-QAEDA IS FORMED

Failing to silence his opposition to pro-Western policies, the Saudis banished bin Laden in 1992 and he moved to Sudan. He gathered together the militant contacts he had made in the Afghan-Soviet war to form al-Qaeda, a jihadist terrorist organization, which he funded from his annual $7 million stipend from his family. The family disowned him and cut off his funds, but he did not falter in his efforts to provoke the United States, the country that he regarded as the greatest enemy of Islam. Soon, he was ready to start his international campaign of terror – in 1996 al-Qaeda blew up US military trucks in Saudi Arabia; in 1997 they killed tourists in Egypt; and in 1998 bin Laden masterminded his most provocative and sophisticated act so far, simultaneously bombing the US embassies in Kenya and Tanzania, killing 300 people.

By then Osama bin Laden had already been exiled from Sudan for his terrorist activities and returned to Afghanistan, where he was given the protection of the Taliban authorities. Deemed to be one of the biggest threats to US security, he was already a wanted man and had often railed publicly against the West, declaring a holy war against America, claiming that it was pillaging the Muslim world and abetting the enemies of Islam.

THE SHOCK OF 9/11

Few took the declaration of war seriously – after all, he was just one man at the head of a small band of followers, while the United States was the greatest military superpower in the world. Then, on 11 September 2001, al-Qaeda committed an act of terrorism that struck right at the heart of America.

Supporters of Jamiat Ulema Islam-Nazaryati shout slogans against the killing of Osama bin Laden.

Bin Laden's followers hijacked four American commercial passenger airliners. Two of the planes were flown at the symbolic and literal pinnacles of US finance corporatism, the Twin Towers of the World Trade Center in New York. The first plane hit the North Tower at 8.46 am and the world watched live television images in horror as the second plane hit the South Tower at 9.03 am. The towers collapsed in a huge billowing cloud of dust and debris that covered miles around. Within the next hour, another plane was flown directly into the Pentagon building, the centre of American military operations at Arlington, Virginia. The passengers of the fourth plane, United Airlines Flight 93, fought the hijackers and the aircraft was brought down, killing everyone on board, before it reached its Washington target. In total, 2,996 people died in the combined attacks on 9/11, including all 19 hijackers. The US, its major institutions and its way of life suddenly seemed impossibly fragile and defenceless in the face of one man's deadly ambition to bring it to its knees. It was bin Laden's finest hour.

THE HUNT FOR BIN LADEN

The US responded with the 'War on Terror'. It immediately formed a military coalition that ousted the Taliban in Afghanistan within months, but bin Laden could not be found and was believed to be hiding in the treacherous border country between Pakistan and Afghanistan. Further al-Qaeda operations followed, and many operatives were killed or captured, but bin Laden remained elusive for nearly ten years. Finally, US President Barack Obama announced that bin Laden had been discovered in a compound in Abbottabad, Pakistan, by US forces and shot dead on 2 May 2011.

This multi-millionaire and architect of a new type of terrorism that had the West trembling in fear was living an apparently simple life in virtual isolation in a walled compound. His legacy haunts the West and its sympathizers, who are continually braced against future attack from his ardent acolytes.

Index

Acknowledgments

We would like to thank the following for the use of their pictures reproduced in this book:

Adam-carr.net
192

Carnavalet Museum
96

defenseimagery.mil
215

Dodmedia
210

German Federal Archives
168

Godfried Warreyn
38

Goodman, from *The Life of Florence Nightingale* **(1913)**
130

The Hungarian National Gallery
32

JCB Archive of Early American Images
84

Karla Bulla
148

Kopengagener Museum
76

Library of Congress
106, 184

Louvre Museum
33

M.H. de Yound Memorial Museum
93

National Archives of Australia
135

The National Archives
164, 183

Shutterstock
16, 24, 29, 50, 58, 67, 80, 103, 110, 118, 122, 127, 152, 157, 160, 172, 176, 191, 197, 205, 219

Source Book Press
144

Städer Museum
70

State Library of Victoria, Melbourne
134

State Museum of Political History of Russia
147

Wikimedia
143, 163

All other photographs and illustrations are the copyright of Quantum Publishing. While every effort has been made to credit contributors, the publisher would like to apologize should there have been any omissions or errors—and would be pleased to make the appropriate correction for future editions of the book.